Rocky Mountain Cooking

Recipes to Bring Canada's Backcountry Home

KATIE MITZEL

appetite

Appetite by Random House® and colophon are registered trademarks of
Penguin Random House LLC.

Library and Archives Canada Cataloguing in Publication is available upon request.

ISBN: 9780147530981
eBook ISBN: 9780147530998

Book design by Five Seventeen
Food Photography and photos on pages i, ii, iii, v, vi, 206 by Shallon Cunningham
Photos on pages viii, 3, 4, 8, 10, 17, 25, 34, 36, 44, 57, 68, 78, 81, 88, 90, 92, 102, 142,
166, 168, 198, 203, 206 by Roger Laurilla
Photos on pages x, 3, 29, 114, 126, 130, 180, 214 by Paul Zizka
Photos on pages 6, 200, 204 by Noel Rogers
Photo on page 32 by Ryan Bavin
Photo on page 66 by Jamieson Caskenette
Photo on page 118 courtesy of Mistaya Lodge
Photo on page 140 by Catalin Mitrache

Printed and bound in China

Published in Canada by Appetite by Random House®,
a division of Penguin Random House LLC.

www.penguinrandomhouse.ca

10 9 8 7 6 5 4 3 2 1

To my family.

Contents

Early Offerings

The Perfect Trail Muffins

Zucchini is an awesome backcountry staple that can be baked, roasted, stuffed, or made into these terrific muffins. These are more than delicious trail treats; they also offer a good pop of energy for that extra trail hike or ski run you hadn't planned on doing!

MAKES 12 MUFFINS

Here's what you'll need:

1½ cups all-purpose flour

½ cup granulated sugar

½ cup packed brown sugar, plus extra for topping

2 teaspoons baking powder

1 teaspoon baking soda

Kosher salt

1 teaspoon ground cinnamon, divided

½ teaspoon ground nutmeg

¼ teaspoon ground ginger

2 eggs

1½ cups peeled, grated zucchini

⅓ cup canola oil

1 teaspoon vanilla extract

Here's how it's done:

1. Preheat your oven to 375°F. Lightly grease a 12-cup muffin tin or line each cup with parchment liners.

2. In a large mixing bowl, combine the flour, both sugars, baking powder, baking soda, and a pinch of salt with ½ teaspoon of the cinnamon, the nutmeg, and ginger. Mix well, making sure there are no lumps of brown sugar.

3. In a small mixing bowl, beat the two eggs. Add the grated zucchini (and any of its residue liquid), oil, and vanilla.

4. Fold the wet ingredients into the dry ingredients, making sure not to overmix (otherwise the muffins will be too dense and heavy).

5. Evenly distribute the batter among the muffin cups; it should sit just below the rim of the cups. Sprinkle some brown sugar and the remaining ½ teaspoon of cinnamon over each uncooked muffin top.

6. Bake on the middle rack of the oven for 30 to 35 minutes, or until the muffins are lightly browned and a cake tester inserted into the center of a muffin comes out clean.

7. Place the muffin pans on a wire rack until cool enough to touch. Let cool for longer if you are saving them for later, or simply tear in half, smother with butter, and eat immediately.

Introduction

Growing up in a large city in Ontario, I often felt I was meant to be somewhere else. It wasn't that I didn't feel a sense of belonging in my hometown; it was more that I had a thirst for the outdoors that I couldn't seem to quench. When I eventually made a few trips out west and found myself surrounded by open meadows, steep mountains, and towering, green forests, I realized I had discovered my true place: a world where the restorative properties of nature were not just an idea but a necessary, concrete part of a happy life.

After a few years at university, doing the things my parents expected of me, I returned to the west with the intention of staying for the summer, getting a cool job, doing some hikes, and trying to live in a way that was more connected to nature. I never left.

After a couple of years of waitressing and working office jobs, I landed a summer job at a backcountry lodge in Banff National Park, which changed my ideas for the future. It showed me that I could make a living doing something I loved, something that was unconventional but that also gave me the opportunity to grow into the person I had always wanted to be: a hiker, a skier, a woodcutter, a water hauler, a problem solver, a backcountry chef, an outdoor person!

I discovered that many people working in the backcountry were a lot like me. They were searching for themselves, seeing if they could live off the grid, and becoming adept at hiking for one-half of the year and skiing the other—and they rejoiced in being a part of the backcountry experience. No one, guests or staff, was focusing on the five-day workweek with its deadlines and curated expectations. That type of approach belonged firmly in the city.

Having said that, working in a backcountry lodge had its own unique challenges. From hiking and skiing five or six hours a day in order to fend off cabin fever, to springing to the rescue when a propane tank needed changing in −40°C (which coincidentally is also −40°F) weather, to shooing off a porcupine that was gnawing on the side of my cabin at 3:00 a.m., I never knew what the day would hold. The one constant was the work, which, admittedly, could be tedious and exhausting—chopping wood by the cord, hauling water by the gallon, cooking gourmet food for large groups without the benefits of power, washing hundreds of dishes a day by hand without running water, marking trails by the half-mile, and greeting guests by the thousands, always with a smile on my face. The immense number of lodge chores, and the colossal physical effort they required, meant this was not a job for the faint of heart. But the rewards never failed to outweigh the sacrifices.

———— ‣•‣ ————

After a few years as a lodge assistant, it was time to try something new. I had developed a passion for food and food preparation when I had previously traveled overseas. I was interested in the organization of the different kitchens I had worked in throughout Europe, the different combinations of textures and seasonings I had tasted in Nepal, and the presentation of food in the other backcountry lodges I had visited. Every chef I worked with taught me some trick of the trade, and with my accumulated knowledge and abundant enthusiasm, I managed to secure a position as a backcountry chef. The objective was to feed calorie-depleted people who had walked a long way to experience the backcountry and its wilderness; if that food was also tasty, it was a bonus. Luckily, backcountry gourmet was what I did best, and I got a kick from developing menus that caught people off guard. I cooked dishes full of unexpected flavors and mouthwatering aromas, using fresh food brought in on horseback, or by helicopter or snowmobile. I couldn't ignore the rush I felt when I heard the oohs and aahs from the guests as they dug in. I had found my niche.

During more than twenty years in the industry, I have worked in some incredible back-country lodges. Every lodge has its own special appeal, but they all offer their guests the prospect of adventure, total immersion in natural beauty, and the option of "unplugging" from daily life. Over the years, I've seen time and time again how a first experience of backcountry lodge living usually marks the beginning of a love affair.

What do I mean by "love affair"? I'm talking about the elation you feel, followed by the most wonderful calm, when you're sitting on top of a mountain in the middle of nowhere. On the way up, you can feel your legs shaking, your lungs burning, and your focus blurring from the strength of the wind. Yet, you keep going, undeterred by elevation or the thought of being able to turn back. Once on top, sitting beside a giant cairn made by everyone who has climbed this peak and added a stone, you feel so proud of yourself and totally aware of your surroundings. The endorphins that are activated after a mountain hike—after any exercise—are all-encompassing and addictive. They make you feel the same as you do after an amazing first date. Many backcountry guests come to the mountains just to experience that feeling of absolute bliss.

My goal with this book is to teach you how to enjoy that feeling of bliss in your own kitchen. No matter where you live, or whether you've visited the backcountry, there are remarkable influences from this environment that you can incorporate into your daily cooking. Think of the mountains, the glacial lakes, the carpets of wildflowers, the boulders covered in emerald green

lichen—these are the palettes that often inspire me in the kitchen. I'm drawn to the endless varieties of color and texture I've encountered during my many hours outdoors, and the memories of them keep me stimulated for hours after I have hung up my hiking boots and placed a gorgeously marinated wild salmon in the oven.

This cookbook contains a collection of diverse and eclectic dishes that I have prepared in many backcountry lodges and huts over the years. You don't have to be a skier or hiker to enjoy them. The majority of ingredients won't require you to seek out a specialty grocery store—you will likely find you have most of them at home or that you already shop for them regularly and have been looking for a different way to prepare them.

Use the recipes to inject a little novelty into your daily life. Start your day with a hearty and warming baked French toast casserole with streusel (page 21) or maybe the skillet-baked huevos rancheros (page 31) instead of boiled egg and toast. Enjoy a fabulous salad paired with crispy fried chicken with buttermilk dipping sauce (page 164) for a late lunch. Indulge a craving for the richness of a halibut steak, cooked to perfection and placed atop a bed of roasted asparagus, with pan-fried scallops and a velvety beurre blanc (page 146), to help you forget your troubles at the end of the day.

I've also included my best bread recipes, as well as a selection of recipes for delicious cakes, an array of baked goodies, and warming soups to keep on hand. I'm sure that, as you leaf through the pages, you will find something—many things—to prepare that will bring your friends and family to the table to share a meal, talk about your day, or maybe plan your next trip to the great outdoors.

The backcountry can seem hostile or vibrant, overwhelming or inspirational, but however you imagine or experience it, its constant reminders to stay present is its best legacy. If you can nurture that sense of being in the moment in your home and kitchen, I suspect that the peace we can gain from all the natural gifts that the backcountry offers will follow close behind.

So what are you waiting for?

Katie Mitzel

Baking at Altitude

I am often asked if baking and cooking at altitude is a challenge. At this point, I've pretty much got it figured out but that wasn't always the case. I can remember some days when I would have to tell my fellow skiers that I couldn't go with them because my cake had exploded in the oven or because my bread was hard as a rock. These aren't great memories, but they're certainly a great incentive to pay attention to the factors affecting these flops. What I have learned from my mistakes is that the higher the altitude, the more pertinent the adjustments to your recipes.

Altitude affects cooking and baking because of thinner air and resulting lower atmospheric pressure that you find at high altitudes. It affects everything from boiling water to baking cakes and bread. The atmosphere is also much drier, so moisture can evaporate from a dish before it's done cooking.

><><

How can this be remedied?

We know that leavening agents like yeast, baking soda and baking powder expand faster at altitude. As a result, we lower the quantities of the leavening agent. It's also important to get into the habit of judging using visual cues—you can check to see if bread dough has risen enough not necessarily by how much time has passed but by checking that the dough has doubled in size.

We also know that because the air is drier at altitude, liquids evaporate faster and the resulting baked goods can wind up with more concentrated sugars. We can make adjustments to recipes by making sure to grease and flour cake pans, slightly lowering the added sugar, increasing the amount of liquid, decreasing baking times, and increasing the oven temperature. The faster cooking time will keep the mixture from rising too much and drying out the ingredients.

continued

A few simple adjustments to your cooking can help you adjust any recipe you like. For the purposes of this book, I've assumed that you're cooking at altitudes below 3,000 feet, but if you're up in the mountains, here are some simple steps to make sure your recipe turns out perfectly each and every time.

For altitudes above 3,000 feet

1. Reduce the leavening agent: for each tablespoon, reduce by ⅛ teaspoon—it might not seem like a lot, but this reduction will keep the recipe from rising too quickly.
2. Reduce the sugar: for each cup, reduce by 1 tablespoon—this will ensure the sugars don't become too concentrated
3. Reduce the oven time: for a full hour, decrease by 10 to 15 minutes, and use visual cues to help indicate doneness
4. Increase the liquid: for each cup used, add 1 to 2 tablespoons
5. Increase the oven temperature by 25°F

For altitudes above 5,000 feet

1. Reduce the leavening agent: for each teaspoon, reduce by a ¼ teaspoon—it might not seem like lot, but this reduction will keep the recipe from rising too quickly
2. Reduce the sugar: for each cup, reduce by 2 tablespoons—this will ensure the sugars don't become too concentrated
3. Reduce the oven time: for a full hour, decrease by 10 to 15 minutes and use visual cues to help indicate doneness
4. Increase the liquid: for each cup used, add 3 to 4 tablespoons
5. Increase the oven temperature by 25°F

For altitudes above 7,000 feet

1. Reduce the leavening agent: for each 1 teaspoon, reduce by ¼ teaspoon—it might not seem like a lot, but this reduction will keep the recipe from rising too quickly
2. Reduce the sugar: for each cup, reduce by 3 tablespoons—this will ensure the sugars don't become too concentrated
3. Reduce the oven time: for a full hour, decrease by 10 to 15 minutes and use visual cues to help indicate doneness
4. Increase the liquid for each cup used, add 4 tablespoons
5. Increase the oven temperature by 25°F

Breakfast Quiche for All

During the off-season from the lodge, my man makes most of our breakfasts. But to him, breakfast is hearty: 20 pancakes, 2 pounds of bacon, and strong coffee. He would never dream of eating a quiche. Until now. Here is a beautiful, elegant quiche that we both devour for a weekend breakfast. It uses a process called blind baking, which makes all quiches a thing of perfection.

SERVES 6

Here's what you'll need:

PASTRY:

1 ½ cups all-purpose flour

¾ teaspoon kosher salt

¼ cup vegetable shortening, cold, cubed

¼ cup unsalted butter, cold, cubed

3–5 tablespoons ice-cold water

FILLING:

1 tablespoon unsalted butter

1 medium white onion, diced

2 garlic cloves, crushed

½ teaspoon kosher salt

Ground black pepper

5 eggs

¾ cup whipping (35–40%) cream

2 cups cubed cooked ham

1 cup grated Swiss cheese

1 cup grated Gruyère cheese

¼ cup grated Parmigiano-Reggiano cheese

1 tablespoon roughly chopped fresh basil leaves (or to taste), plus extra for garnish

1 teaspoon ground nutmeg

3 green onions, for garnish

Here's how it's done:

1. To make the pastry, in a large mixing bowl, combine the flour and salt. Add the shortening and mix with a wooden spoon. Using two forks or a pastry cutter, cut in the butter. Work it in until you have a crumbly mess. You are looking for pea-size pieces of both the fats. Add the water, 1 tablespoon at a time, mixing well after each addition to incorporate and working it in with a stiff spatula or wooden spoon. You may not need all of the water. You want just enough to encourage the dough to stick together when pressed.

2. Place a large sheet of parchment or waxed paper on your work surface. Tip the dough onto the paper. Using your hands, flatten the dough a bit and then fold it five or six times to incorporate any dry bits of flour, using the parchment paper to help you bring it together. Work quickly—you want the dough to stay as cold as possible, without your body heat melting the fats.

3. Flatten the dough to about 1-inch thick and wrap it in plastic wrap. Refrigerate for at least 30 minutes, or up to overnight.

4. If you've chilled the dough overnight, remove it from the fridge 10 to 12 minutes before working with it again. If the dough was in the fridge for only 30 minutes or so, you can use it immediately.

5. Preheat the oven to 375°F. Butter a 9-inch pie dish.

6. On a lightly floured work surface, roll out the dough, moving it constantly to prevent it from sticking. The finished dough should be ⅛-inch thick and about 12 inches in diameter—slightly larger than the pie dish to allow for crimping.

recipe continues

7. Roll the dough around a rolling pin and unwind it over the prepared pie dish, allowing it to hang over the sides. Crimp the sides and put about eight small fork punctures in the bottom of the crust. Place a large piece of parchment paper over the bottom and sides of the crust to cover them.

8. Pour some blind baking weights or dried beans over the parchment and bake for about 20 minutes, or until the edges of the crust start to brown. Remove the weights and bake for 10 to 12 minutes longer, until the bottom crust has turned golden brown. Blind baking the crust means it doesn't get soggy. Once it is baked, place the pie dish on a wire rack and let cool for at least 10 minutes. Leave the oven switched on.

9. While the crust is blind baking, prepare the filling. In a saucepan over medium heat, melt the butter. Add the onion and garlic and sauté for about 5 to 6 minutes, or until softened. Season with the salt and pepper to taste.

10. In a mixing bowl, whisk the eggs. Pour in the cream and mix well. Add the ham, the three cheeses, basil, nutmeg, and the cooked onion and garlic. Mix to combine all the ingredients.

11. Pour the egg mixture into the cooled pie crust. Bake on the middle rack of the oven for about 35 to 40 minutes, or until the edges of the quiche have set but there is still a slight jiggle in the center.

12. Let stand for a few minutes before serving so it is easier to cut. Sprinkle some basil and the green onions overtop, if desired. Now cut your loved one a generous wedge.

Scrambled Muffins with Savory Cheese and Chives

Anyone who has spent any time in backcountry lodges knows the eggie weggie tradition. It has transcended the most popular of breakfast legends to become one in its own right. With these scrambled muffins, I have created a close cousin to the infamous eggie weggie. Don't worry though, eggie weggie, we will always love you!

MAKES 12 MUFFINS

Here's what you'll need:

12 eggs

½ cup whipping (35–40%) cream

Kosher salt and ground black pepper

½ cup chopped prosciutto or deli ham

2 tablespoons chopped fresh chives

½ red bell pepper, chopped

5 cremini mushrooms, chopped

1 cup grated aged cheddar cheese

Here's how it's done:

1. Preheat the oven to 350°F. Lightly grease a 12-cup muffin tin or line each cup with parchment liners.

2. In a small measuring cup, gently whisk the eggs. Whisk in the cream without creating a foam. Season to taste with salt and pepper.

3. Evenly distribute the prosciutto, chives, bell pepper, and mushrooms between the muffin cups. Place the cheese on top. Carefully pour the egg and cream mixture into each muffin cup to just below the rim.

4. Bake on the middle rack of the oven for 20 to 25 minutes, or until a cake tester inserted into the center of a muffin comes out clean.

5. Let stand for a couple of minutes and then pop the scrambled egg muffins out of their tin and onto a serving plate.

Pumpkin Spice Pancakes

Pancake breakfasts are always very popular at lodges, and these particular pancakes make a terrific trail goody. The smooth texture of the puréed pumpkin also adds a bit of a fun palate teaser to a well-loved breakfast staple.

SERVES 6

Here's what you'll need:

1½ cups all-purpose flour

3 tablespoons granulated sugar

2 teaspoons baking powder

½ teaspoon kosher salt

½ teaspoon ground cinnamon

½ teaspoon ground nutmeg

¼ teaspoon ground cloves

¼ teaspoon ground ginger

1 egg

½ cup pumpkin purée

1 cup buttermilk

2 tablespoons unsalted butter, melted

Here's how it's done:

1. In a large bowl, whisk together the flour, sugar, baking powder, salt, cinnamon, nutmeg, cloves, and ginger.

2. In another mixing bowl, whisk the egg. Add the pumpkin purée, followed by the buttermilk and butter, whisking between each addition to combine.

3. Fold the wet ingredients into the dry ingredients. Mix until blended but not overmixed.

4. Heat a skillet or griddle over medium heat. Use shortening or a nonstick spray to lightly coat the griddle. Reapply as necessary to avoid sticking.

5. Preheat the oven to 225°F. Place a wire rack over a baking sheet and set it on the middle rack of the oven.

6. To cook the pancakes, pour about ¼ cup of batter onto the griddle. Cook each pancake for 2 minutes per side, or until both sides are golden brown and cooked through. Repeat with the remaining batter, wrapping the cooked pancakes loosely in aluminum foil and keeping them warm in the oven.

NOTE: This recipe doubles beautifully if you want to make cheese dudes for the kids' lunches or for your ski trip or trail hike. And what are they you ask? Cheese dudes are two cold pancakes sandwiched together with cream cheese and jam (we like raspberry) and cut into four.

Baked French Toast Casserole with Streusel

This is the one breakfast dish you must make when the kids have a lazy weekend planned and you have time to kick back and enjoy your first meal of the day. If you want to take this to the next level, grab some whipped cream and maple syrup. (Note that you have to prep this the night before you plan to eat it.)

SERVES 6

Here's what you'll need:

STREUSEL TOPPING:

¼ cup unsalted butter, softened

¾ cup all-purpose flour

1 cup chopped pecans (optional)

¾ cup granulated sugar

1½ teaspoons ground cinnamon

FRENCH TOAST CASSEROLE:

8 eggs

2½ cups 2% milk

½ cup granulated sugar

1 tablespoon vanilla extract

½ teaspoon ground nutmeg

½ teaspoon ground cinnamon

Kosher salt

12 cups cubed hearty bread

TO SERVE:

1½ cups whipped cream (optional)

Maple syrup (optional)

Here's how it's done:

1. To make the streusel topping, in a medium bowl, and using a pastry cutter or two knives, cut the butter into the flour. Add the pecans (if using), sugar, and cinnamon and stir. Add 1 tablespoon of water, working it in with a stiff spatula or wooden spoon until you have a crumbly dough. (This can also be done in a food processor on pulse.) Place in the fridge, uncovered, to chill for at least 1 hour, or up to overnight.

2. To make the casserole, whisk the eggs in a large bowl. Add the milk and whisk to incorporate. Add the sugar, vanilla, nutmeg, cinnamon, and a pinch of salt. Mix to combine.

3. Place the bread cubes in a 13- x 9-inch baking dish and pour the egg mixture overtop, making sure the whole shebang is well coated. Cover and refrigerate overnight.

4. In the morning, preheat the oven to 350°F.

5. Lightly mix the casserole with a wooden spoon and then scatter the streusel topping evenly overtop.

6. Bake on the middle rack of the oven for about 50 minutes, until the streusel is browned and bubbly and the casserole is showing no signs of wobbling.

7. Serve with a dollop of whipped cream or maple syrup—or both!—if you like.

Mini Apple Strudels

I used to be intimidated by any kind of baking that involved puff pastry. How could I even imagine working with a pastry that would miraculously "puff" on its own? Well, I now love working with puff pastry, as it is unfathomably easy to use as well as gorgeous and flaky. This recipe pairs it with Granny Smith apples to create a simple breakfast strudel that looks great, smells divine, and tastes brilliant.

MAKES 6 PASTRIES

Here's what you'll need:

2 sheets of store-bought all-butter puff pastry (see note)

1¼ cups cored and cubed Granny Smith apples, skin on

3 tablespoons demerara sugar

1 teaspoon ground cinnamon

¼ teaspoon ground nutmeg

¼ teaspoon ground cloves

½ cup golden raisins, covered in room-temperature water

1 egg, beaten + 1 tablespoon water, for egg wash

1½ tablespoons sanding sugar or similar coarse sugar

1 cup icing sugar (optional)

½ teaspoon vanilla extract (optional)

1–2 tablespoons whole or 2% milk (optional)

Here's how it's done:

1. Remove the puff pastry from the freezer and refrigerate overnight, or thaw on the countertop for about 45 minutes.

2. In a mixing bowl, toss the apples with the demerara sugar, cinnamon, nutmeg, and cloves. Drain the raisins well, discarding the water. Add them to the mixing bowl and mix to combine. Set aside.

3. On a lightly floured work surface, roll out the puff pastry slightly to get a 18- × 12-inch rectangle and remove any bumps or bubbles. Don't overwork it. Cut the pastry into six 6-inch squares. Repeat with the second sheet.

4. Line a baking tray with parchment paper.

5. Brush the perimeter of each pastry square with the egg wash, leaving the center dry. Place about a tablespoon of the apple mixture in the middle of each pastry, leaving the outer edges bare. You may have some left over apple mixture, which is fine. Place a second piece of pastry on top, lining it up with the bottom piece. Crimp the edges with a fork, all the way around, to seal the package.

6. Place each bundle on the prepared baking tray as you complete them, giving yourself adequate space to work. It is easier to lift the pastry if you use a spatula lightly coated in flour.

7. Using a lame or razor, lightly score three small slits across the top of each pastry. Brush all the strudels with the remaining egg wash and sprinkle generously with sanding sugar. Place the baking tray, uncovered, in the freezer for about 10 minutes.

8. Meanwhile, preheat the oven to 425°F.

9. Bake the strudels for 10 minutes, and then turn down the heat to 375°F and bake for 10 more minutes, or until the pastry is beautifully puffed and a wonderful golden brown. You aren't going for dark brown, so if you feel they are ready before the timer goes off, simply take them out.

10. Transfer the strudels to a wire rack to cool for about 12 to 15 minutes.

11. If you would like icing on top, mix the icing sugar with the vanilla in a small bowl. Stir in the milk, 1 tablespoon at a time, until you get the desired consistency. If you feel it is setting up too quickly, just add a bit more milk to lighten it.

NOTE: When you're working with all-butter puff pastry, cook it at a constant high heat. The steam created is what makes the pastry puff, so don't be tempted to open the oven door to check it out.

Powder Snow Breakfast Casserole

Some mornings, it is nice to have a go-to breakfast that takes the challenge out of having to impress family and friends. This is ideal for those mornings. You'll soon know it off by heart, and it can be put together with groceries you probably keep on hand. (Note that you have to prep this the night before you plan to eat it.)

SERVES 4–6

Here's what you'll need:

6 cups cubed brioche or French bread

½ cup chopped ham or sausage

1 cup shredded aged cheddar cheese

1 (4.5 oz) can chopped green chilies, drained

8 eggs

1½ cups 2% milk

1 tablespoon smooth Dijon mustard

Kosher salt and ground black pepper

2 green onions, chopped

Here's how it's done:

1. Grease a 13- × 9-inch baking dish.

2. In a large mixing bowl, combine the bread with the ham, cheese, and chilies. Pour this mixture into the prepared baking dish.

3. In a separate large bowl, whisk the eggs. Add the milk, mustard, and a pinch each of salt and pepper. Whisk to incorporate and then pour over the bread mixture. Make sure the bread is saturated and there are no dry bits poking up. Cover tightly with plastic wrap so it doesn't sink into the casserole. Refrigerate overnight and go play some Yahtzee or watch *Corner Gas* with the kids. You're done for the night!

4. The next morning, remove the casserole from the fridge about 30 minutes before you plan to bake it. Preheat the oven to 350°F.

5. Remove the plastic wrap from the casserole and bake on the middle rack of the oven for 45 minutes. If it is still a tad jiggly, keep it in the oven for another 10 to 15 minutes. Let stand for a couple of minutes before serving. Serve with a generous sprinkle of chopped green onions overtop.

Salted Caramel Buns

Salted caramel is sweeping the backcountry and I am totally jumping on that train. There is something so incredibly decadent about the union of sweet and salty that I just can't put into words. Instead, I simply embrace it. In this recipe, it is best to use a coarse sea salt. The visual effect is nearly as wonderful as the tasting experience. (Note that you might prefer to prep these the night before you plan to eat them.)

MAKES 12 BUNS

Here's what you'll need:

BREAD:

¼ cup granulated sugar

½ cup tap-hot water

1 tablespoon active dry yeast

2 eggs, beaten

½ cup 2% milk

¼ cup salted butter

1 teaspoon kosher salt

4½ cups all-purpose flour, divided

CARAMEL SYRUP:

½ cup salted butter

1 cup packed brown sugar

¼ cup light corn syrup

FILLING:

⅓ cup granulated sugar

2 teaspoons ground cinnamon

Sea salt

2–3 tablespoons salted butter, softened

TOPPING:

Coarse sea salt

Here's how it's done:

1. For these buns, you can prepare your bread the night before and leave it in the fridge overnight. Otherwise you can start bright and early and catch a little tv or radio or go back to bed and read your book for an hour—oh, options!

2. In a large mixing bowl, dissolve the sugar in the water. Sprinkle the yeast in, stir very gently, and then let the mixture sit for about 8 to 10 minutes. When the yeast is bubbly and frothy, it is ready.

3. Add the eggs, milk, butter, and salt and mix to combine. Add 4 cups of the flour, 1 cup at a time, mixing with a wooden spoon between each addition to incorporate.

4. Using your hands, form the dough into a uniform ball, catching any dough strands and tucking them back in.

5. Dust your work surface with some of the remaining ½ cup of flour and tip the dough onto your work surface. Using both hands, knead the dough. Press the center of the dough with the heels of your hands, then push them onto the dough and away from you. Using quarter turns, pull the dough back toward you with the heels of your hands, adding only enough extra flour to keep the dough from sticking. Continue this process until you begin to feel air developing in the dough and it is smooth and springs back when poked with your finger. This whole process should take between 8 and 10 minutes.

6. Lightly oil a large mixing bowl, place the dough in it, turning once to ensure the whole ball is covered in oil, and cover with a tea towel. Set aside in a warm, draft-free spot to rise for up to 1 hour or until it has doubled in size.

recipe continues

7. After the dough has risen, gently punch it down in the bowl and knead it again on a lightly floured work surface for about 8 minutes. Add a dusting of flour to the rolling pin to prevent any sticking. Roll the dough into an 18- × 10-inch rectangle that is ¾-inch thick. The key is to create an even surface.

8. Grease a 17- × 11-inch roasting pan.

9. To make the syrup, in a medium saucepan over medium-low heat, gently melt the butter. Add the brown sugar and whisk it into the butter. Increase the heat to medium, add the corn syrup and continue to cook, stirring constantly, until it reaches a boil. Boil for only 30 seconds and then remove from the heat. Pour this sauce into the bottom of the prepared roasting pan. Set aside.

10. To make the filling, place the sugar, cinnamon, and a pinch of sea salt in a mixing bowl and mix to combine.

11. Using an offset spatula, spread the butter over the dough, leaving about a 1-inch-wide margin on the long end farthest from you free of butter.

12. Sprinkle the sugar mixture generously over the butter.

13. Starting at the long end closest to you, roll the rectangle tightly into an even cylinder. Pinch the seam so it is well sealed, and roll the dough over once onto itself to make sure it is tight. Using a serrated knife or unwaxed dental floss, cut 12 evenly sized buns.

14. Place the buns flat on the caramel syrup, leaving about ¼ inch between each one so there is room to rise. Cover with a clean tea towel and let rise in a warm, draft-free spot for 30 to 40 minutes.

15. Halfway through the rising time, preheat the oven to 350°F.

16. Bake the buns on the middle rack of the oven for about 30 minutes, or until the tops are golden brown and the buns sound hollow when tapped.

17. Let the buns cool in the pan for 15 minutes before inverting onto a serving platter. Using a spatula, gather the remaining syrup to drizzle overtop.

18. Finish with a hearty sprinkling of coarse sea salt—as much or as little as you like. The combination is irresistible!

Skillet-Baked Huevos Rancheros

Hearty breakfasts are par for the course in backcountry lodges. Folks are out on the trail all day and need a terrific start to keep them energized until they pause for lunch. This breakfast checks all the boxes for a busy morning and will most certainly keep you at the head of the pack.

SERVES 6

Here's what you'll need:

½ cup canned kidney beans, drained and rinsed

½ cup canned black beans, drained and rinsed

½ cup canned pinto beans, drained and rinsed

2 tablespoons extra virgin olive oil, divided

1 (2-inch-long) jalapeño, seeded and diced

1 (28 oz) can whole plum tomatoes

1 small white onion, diced

3 garlic cloves, minced

1 cup fresh cilantro, plus extra for serving

Kosher salt

1 teaspoon chili powder

1 teaspoon Spanish paprika

1 teaspoon ground cumin

1 teaspoon ground coriander

2 tablespoons red wine vinegar

1 tablespoon granulated sugar

2 ripe Roma tomatoes, cut into wedges

6 whole eggs

1 cup grated Monterey Jack cheese

1–2 tablespoons vegetable oil

6 (each 6-inch) corn tortillas

Sour cream, for serving

1 large avocado, pitted and sliced, for serving

Lime wedges

Here's how it's done:

1. Preheat the oven to 375°F.

2. Place all the beans in a bowl and set aside.

3. In a large skillet or cast iron pan over medium heat, place 1 tablespoon of the oil and the beans. Add the jalapeño, mix everything together, bring to a simmer, and cook for 5 to 6 minutes, stirring occasionally.

4. Place the remaining 1 tablespoon of oil in a food processor along with the tomatoes and their juice, the onion, garlic, cilantro, and a pinch of salt. Blend until smooth. Let sit for 1 minute.

5. Add the tomato mix to the beans, followed by the chili powder, paprika, cumin, and coriander. Mix to combine. Add the vinegar and sugar and mix well. Arrange the tomato wedges in the mixture and turn off the heat.

6. Crack the eggs right into the skillet on top of the tomato and beans, leaving a bit of space between them. Sprinkle with the cheese and bake on the middle rack of the oven for 15 to 20 minutes, or until the eggs are cooked to your desired doneness.

7. While the eggs cook, place the oil in a clean skillet over medium-low heat and heat the corn tortillas, one at a time, for about 30 to 40 seconds per side. Wrap in aluminum foil to keep warm.

8. Place a warmed tortilla on a plate and serve with a large helping of the bean mixture and 1 egg. Serve with cilantro, sour cream, avocado, and a lime wedge on the side.

Assiniboine Lodge

One of my fondest memories of Assiniboine Lodge is of the Aurora Borealis. I was snug in my lodge bed when I was suddenly awoken around 4:00 a.m. by an exhilarated Ken Jones—a veritable jack-of-all-trades lodge colleague—who, outside of my lodge quarters, kept saying, "Well, I'll be" over and over again. We soon found ourselves out front alongside him with our jackets and toques on, stunned by a glorious, jaw-dropping Northern Lights display—a display that, to this day, is still unmatched.

Assiniboine Lodge has always been a beacon in its own way. Surrounded by larch trees, carpets of wildflowers, and stunning lakes paired with Mount Assiniboine standing guard over Assiniboine Provincial Park, you really can't find a more stunning location for a backcountry lodge.

Built in 1927, Assiniboine Lodge was the first backcountry ski lodge in the Canadian Rockies. It was founded by an intrepid group of adventurers, including the Marqui degli Albizzi, an Italian nobleman, and Erling Strom, a Norwegian ski instructor, who fell in love with the Park. Strom himself declared it "the most beautiful valley that one could imagine." It was where he wanted to spend the rest of his life, which he did.

Over the years, Strom and the Assiniboine Lodge team hosted many of Canada's legendary mountain pioneers, such as Ken Jones, the first Canadian-born mountain guide, his wife, Bridget Jones, Lizzie

Rummel, who received the Order of Canada for her contributions to early backcountry lodges, Hans Gmoser, the father of heli-skiing, and Chic Scott, an Alberta-born mountaineer and author, to name a few.

After Strom's tenure, Sepp and Barb Renner, along with their son, Andre, and daughters, Sara and Natalie, operated the lodge for 27 years. It was then passed onto Andre Renner and his partners Claude Duchesne and Annick Blouin, who, in conjunction with BC Parks, completed a rehabilitation and renovation of Assiniboine Lodge.

Today Assiniboine Lodge retains its rustic charm and welcoming spirit. It is accessible by helicopter, hiking, or skiing. Once there you can take advantage of the thoughtfully guided hikes in the summer, and phenomenal ski touring with a professionally certified guide in the winter.

After a day out in Mother Nature, you can find guests sharing stories over tea goodies or hearty homemade meals, or fireside before tucking themselves in under cozy goose-down duvets as the stars fill the nighttime sky (and perhaps before the Northern Lights have everyone scrambling to their windows).

With all its history and rustic charm, Assiniboine is a place to disconnect from the busy world and reconnect with nature, family, and friends—to find peace amongst the mountains.

Tea Time and Goodies

Chocolate with Chocolate on Chocolate Salted Cookies

Yup! You read it right, folks. Double chocolate chip cookies dipped in chocolate and finished with coarse salt. It might be a good idea to double this recipe because, honestly, these little wonders won't last long—especially if you are arming yourselves with them for an afternoon of fishing.

MAKES 2 DOZEN COOKIES

Here's what you'll need:

1 cup salted butter, softened

¾ cup granulated sugar

2 eggs, beaten

3 tablespoons 2% milk

1 teaspoon vanilla extract

2 cups all-purpose flour

⅔ cup cocoa powder

1 teaspoon baking soda

¾ teaspoon kosher salt

2 cups semisweet chocolate chips, divided

1 cup dark chocolate chips

¾ cup whipping (35–40%) cream

Coarse salt

Here's how it's done:

1. Preheat the oven to 350°F. Line a baking sheet with parchment paper or lightly grease with vegetable oil or nonstick spray.

2. Using a handheld or stand mixer, beat the butter with the sugar until pale and fluffy. Add the eggs, milk, and vanilla and mix well.

3. In a separate bowl, mix together the flour, cocoa powder, baking soda, and salt. Add these dry ingredients to the wet ingredients and mix to combine, making sure to not overwork the dough. Fold in 1 cup of the semisweet chocolate chips and all the dark chocolate chips.

4. Using a small ice cream scoop or tablespoon, dollop the cookie dough onto the prepared baking sheet and press gently with a fork. Leave about 1 inch between each cookie.

5. Bake the cookies for 10 to 12 minutes, or until the edges are dry and the middles are still a bit soft and slightly puffy. They will deflate when they cool. Transfer the cookies from the baking sheet to a wire rack to cool completely.

6. Meanwhile, line a cool baking sheet with parchment paper.

7. In a small saucepan over low heat, gently warm the cream. Place the remaining 1 cup of semisweet chocolate chips in a small bowl. When the cream begins to steam a bit and is nearly at a boil, pour it over the chocolate chips. Allow the chocolate to melt under the heat of the cream and then whisk until smooth. It should be warm but not hot.

8. Dip the cooled cookies, one at a time, into the melted chocolate and cream mixture. I dip so it looks like a half moon. You can also use a spoon to drizzle the chocolate overtop if you aren't a keen dipper. Nudge off any excess chocolate with a toothpick or leave it be—what could possibly go wrong? Place the dipped cookies on the prepared baking sheet. While the chocolate is still a bit wet and sticky, sprinkle the coarse salt overtop to add an interesting texture.

9. You can store these cookies for up to 1 week in the fridge, in an airtight container in single layers, separated by parchment or waxed paper.

White Chocolate and Lemon Cookies

This recipe is a bit more on the sophisticated side, with its combination of sweet white chocolate and tart lemon. Take these on a spring ski along with a fruit and cheese basket and a nice thermos of honey tea!

MAKES 2 DOZEN COOKIES

Here's what you'll need:

¾ cup salted butter, softened

½ cup packed brown sugar

¼ cup granulated sugar

1 egg

1 tablespoon lemon juice

2 teaspoons grated lemon zest

1½ cups all-purpose flour

¾ teaspoon baking soda

½ teaspoon kosher salt

2 cups white chocolate chips

Here's how it's done:

1. Preheat the oven to 350°F. Line two baking sheets with parchment paper.

2. Using a handheld or stand mixer, beat the butter with both sugars, making sure there are no lumps in the brown sugar. Beat until fluffy, about 3 minutes. Mix in the egg, followed by the lemon juice and zest.

3. In a separate bowl, mix together the flour, baking soda, and salt.

4. Add the wet ingredients to the dry ingredients. Using a spatula or wooden spoon, mix until the dough feels pliable. Fold in the white chocolate chips until they no longer fall out of the dough.

5. Using an ice cream scoop or a tablespoon, place the cookies on the prepared baking sheets, about 1½ inches apart.

6. Bake one tray at a time on the center rack of the oven for 10 to 12 minutes, or until the edges turn golden brown and the middles are soft and slightly puffy. (If you're baking both trays at once, place one on the top rack and one on the bottom rack and swap their positions halfway through baking time.) Remove the cookies from the oven and let them sit on the baking tray for a couple of minutes.

7. Using a spatula, transfer the cookies to a wire rack to cool completely. They will keep well in an airtight container or resealable bag for 1 week if you don't eat them all the day you make them!

Climbers' Cookies with Cinnamon

This cookie is a great option for taking along with you on any outdoor pursuit, no matter where you need to be: side of a cliff, top of a ski run, bottom of a waterfall. Bring along a batch to share with your companions and to take the edge off when the hike back is still an hour long and the rest of your food ran out miles ago!

MAKES 2 DOZEN COOKIES

Here's what you'll need:

1 cup salted butter, softened

¾ cup packed brown sugar

½ cup granulated sugar

1 egg

2 teaspoons vanilla extract

2 cups all-purpose flour

1½ cups quick oats

1 teaspoon baking soda

1 teaspoon kosher salt

1 teaspoon ground cinnamon

½ teaspoon ground nutmeg

¼ teaspoon ground ginger

Here's how it's done:

1. Preheat the oven to 350°F. Line two baking sheets with parchment paper.

2. Using a handheld or stand mixer, beat the butter with both sugars, making sure there are no lumps in the brown sugar. Beat until fluffy, about 3 minutes. Mix in the egg, followed by the vanilla.

3. In a separate mixing bowl, mix together the flour, oats, baking soda, salt, cinnamon, nutmeg, and ginger.

4. Add the dry ingredients to the wet ingredients in two additions, mixing on low between additions. Scrape down the sides of the bowl and use a spatula to lift up any cookie dough stuck to the bottom. Continue to mix until there are no streaks of flour and all the ingredients are well incorporated. Add a little more flour if the dough is too sticky.

5. Using an ice cream scoop or tablespoon, place the cookies on the prepared baking sheets, about 1½ inches apart.

6. Bake one tray at a time on the center rack of the oven for 10 to 12 minutes, or until the edges are golden and dry. (If you're baking both trays at once, place one on the top rack and one on the bottom rack and swap their positions halfway through baking time.) They may rise a bit but they'll deflate once they have cooled. Using a spatula, transfer the cookies to a wire rack to cool completely.

7. You can store these in an airtight container or resealable bag for up to 1 week.

Poached Bosc Pears

The Bosc pear is a thing of beauty, with its elegant, elongated neck, cinnamon-colored skin, and earthy and aromatic bouquet. They are the best choice for poaching with their easy-to-peel skin and a flesh that holds its shape well. A true delight on any backcountry menu.

SERVES 4

Here's what you'll need:

1½ cups granulated sugar

1 cup dry white wine

4 whole star anise or ¾ teaspoon star anise seeds

1 cinnamon stick

1-inch piece ginger, peeled and quartered lengthwise

4 whole cloves

2 tablespoons vanilla extract or 1 whole pod

1 orange, zested and juiced

4 Bosc pears

3 tablespoons Grand Marnier (optional)

Here's how it's done:

1. In a large saucepan over medium-high heat, whisk the sugar with 3 cups of water and the white wine and bring to a rolling boil. Turn down the heat to medium and add the star anise, cinnamon stick, ginger slices, whole cloves, vanilla, and orange zest and juice. Bring to a simmer.

2. Peel the pears with a very sharp peeler, making sure to keep the neck and stem intact. Slice a sliver off the bottom of each pear to create a flat surface.

3. Turn down the heat to medium-low and place the pears, upright, in the liquid. They should be fully submerged. Poach the pears, uncovered, for 15 to 20 minutes, or until a cake tester can easily glide into the flesh without force. You do not want an undercooked pear. However, a mushy pear will not be a pleasant eating experience either.

4. Remove the pan from the heat and let the pears cool in the poaching liquid. Whey they are just cool enough to touch, using rubber tongs, remove the pears from the liquid, allowing any excess to drip back into the saucepan. Place on a serving plate and put in the fridge, uncovered.

5. Meanwhile, pour the poaching liquid through a sieve and into a clean saucepan. Discard the seasonings. Add the Grand Marnier (if using). Warm the liquid over medium heat, letting it reduce by half so that you have a gorgeous, pecan-colored syrup, about 20 to 30 minutes.

6. Remove the cold pears from the fridge. Plate together or individually. Pour some of the syrup overtop—it is equally good warm or at room temperature.

Carrot Cake with Toasted Coconut

Star gazing and carrot cake are a match made in heaven. Evenings out under the Milky Way can get chilly. The perfect antidote is a hot mug of tea with a slice of scrumptious carrot cake at your side. Making a wish on that shooting star just got a whole lot yummier.

SERVES 12

Here's what you'll need:

CAKE:

3 cups all-purpose flour

2 teaspoons baking soda

2 teaspoons baking powder

1½ teaspoons ground cinnamon

1 teaspoon ground ginger

1 teaspoon ground nutmeg

½ teaspoon ground cloves

1 cup granulated sugar

1 cup packed brown sugar

1 teaspoon kosher salt

4 eggs

1¼ cups canola oil

1 teaspoon vanilla extract

3 cups grated carrot

½ cup chopped walnuts

2–3 cups shredded sweetened coconut

CREAM CHEESE ICING:

1 (8 oz) package cream cheese

½ cup unsalted butter, softened and cubed

1 teaspoon vanilla extract

1¼ cups icing sugar

¼ cup whipping (35–40%) cream

1½ teaspoons grated orange zest

Here's how it's done:

1. Preheat the oven to 350°F. Grease every nook and cranny of a 9-inch springform pan. Line the bottom with parchment paper.

2. To make the cake, in a large mixing bowl, combine the flour, baking soda, and baking powder. Add the cinnamon, ginger, nutmeg, and cloves and mix to combine. Add both sugars, making sure there are no lumps in the brown sugar. Add the salt.

3. In a separate bowl, whisk the eggs until beaten but not frothy. Add the canola oil and vanilla and mix well to combine. Fold in the carrots and walnuts. Use a spatula to fold these wet ingredients into the dry until well combined but not overworked. Pour the batter into the prepared pan.

4. Bake on the middle rack of the oven for 50 to 60 minutes, or until a cake tester inserted into the center comes out clean and the cake has a gorgeous golden hue to it. Let the cake cool completely in the pan on a wire rack before releasing from the pan. Leave the oven switched on.

5. Spread the coconut evenly on a baking tray and toast in the oven for 6 to 8 minutes. Shredded coconut toasts quickly and can burn in the blink of an eye, so be sure to stir occasionally and remove it from the oven as soon as it turns a beautiful golden brown. Set aside to cool.

6. To make the frosting, use a handheld or stand mixer to beat the cream cheese until it is smooth and fluffy. Add the butter, one cube at a time, and beat until smooth. Add the vanilla and all the icing sugar and beat for 2 minutes. Add the cream, mix well, and fold in the orange zest. Refrigerate the frosting, uncovered, for 15 to 20 minutes.

7. Use an offset spatula to frost the cake. Sprinkle the toasted coconut overtop of the frosted cake.

Lemony Lavender Buttermilk Cake

This is a no-fuss, big-taste cake. It also makes an unbelievable companion in a meadow of wildflowers while you're doing a watercolor painting. The lemon-buttermilk drizzle and gorgeous lavender will reflect the colors around you and inspire you to paint some more.

SERVES 12–14

Here's what you'll need:

CAKE:

2 teaspoons organic lavender buds

2 cups + 3 tablespoons granulated sugar, divided

3 cups all-purpose flour

1 tablespoon baking powder

1 teaspoon fine sea salt

1 cup salted butter, softened

3 eggs

1½ teaspoons lemon zest

1 teaspoon vanilla extract

1¼ cups buttermilk

LEMON DRIZZLE:

2 tablespoons buttermilk

1 teaspoon lemon juice

1¼ cups icing sugar

TOPPING:

1 tablespoon cane sugar

1 teaspoon organic lavender buds

1 lemon, zested into long strips

1 teaspoon lemon juice

Lavender sprigs

Here's how it's done:

1. Preheat the oven to 350°F. Grease every nook and cranny of a 9-inch springform pan.

2. If you have never worked with lavender, don't worry. I've learned that essential oils infuse better if you blend them with sugar, so blend the lavender buds with 3 tablespoons of the sugar in a coffee mill or grinder.

3. To make the cake, in a mixing bowl, mix together the ground lavender-sugar blend, flour, baking powder, and salt.

4. Using a handheld or stand mixer, beat the butter until smooth. Add the remaining 2 cups of sugar and beat until pale and fluffy. With the mixer running, add the eggs one at a time, beating well between each addition. Add the lemon zest and vanilla and mix. Add half of the flour mixture and mix on medium speed for a couple of minutes, just to combine. Add the buttermilk in one addition, beating until mixed in. Add the rest of the flour mixture. Mix for 1 full minute, scraping down the sides of the bowl as required.

5. Pour the batter into the prepared pan and bake on the center rack of the oven for 50 to 55 minutes, or until the cake is pulling slightly away from the sides of the pan and a cake tester inserted into the center comes out clean.

6. Let the cake cool completely in the pan on a wire rack before releasing from the pan.

7. To make the lemon drizzle, in a medium bowl, use a fork to whisk the buttermilk and lemon juice with the icing sugar. Place the cooled cake on a serving plate and pour the lemon drizzle overtop the cake, letting it travel down the sides.

8. To make the topping, grind the cane sugar and lavender buds in a coffee mill or grinder. Transfer to a small bowl and mix with the strips of lemon and lemon juice. Toss everything around a bit with your hand and place the lemon strips on top of the cake or on individually cut pieces. Add a few lavender sprigs for a delightful finish.

Individual Pavlovas

There are a lot of wonderful desserts out there (talk about stating the obvious!), but few can hold a torch to the iconic pavlova, a meringue-based dessert served with fresh cream and berries. It is super easy to prepare and assemble, but so impressive that I bet your guests will think otherwise.

MAKES 14–16 PAVLOVAS

Here's what you'll need:

MERINGUE:

5 egg whites, at room temperature

1½ cups superfine sugar

2 teaspoons cornstarch

Kosher salt

½ tablespoon lemon juice

½ tablespoon vanilla extract

CREAM:

1½ cups whipping (35–40%) cream

2 tablespoons icing sugar

1 teaspoon vanilla extract

TOPPING:

Choose from:

3 kiwis, peeled and sliced

6 strawberries, sliced

½ cup blueberries

½ cup blackberries

½ cup raspberries

7–8 gooseberries, halved

Here's how it's done:

1. Prepare a stand mixer by carefully and thoroughly cleaning the bowl and whisk attachment. Line two 18- × 13-inch baking sheets with parchment paper.

2. Double-check the egg whites to make sure there is no trace of yolk.

3. Beat the egg whites on medium speed until stiff peaks start to form, about 1 to 2 minutes. With the machine still running on medium, add the sugar, 1 tablespoon at a time. Once all the sugar has been added, beat for another 3 to 4 minutes. Fold in the cornstarch. Gradually increase the speed of the mixer until it is at medium-high. With the machine running, add a pinch of salt, and then drizzle in the lemon juice, followed by the vanilla. Beat until the mixture is thick and glossy with firm peaks.

4. Dab a pinch of meringue under each corner of the parchment paper on the baking sheets. This will hold down the parchment.

5. Draw circles on the parchment paper, about 4 to 5 inches in diameter. Using two spoons or a piping bag with an open star tip, scoop the meringue mix into the circles, working from the middle outward. You should have 14 to 16 meringues. Using the back of a spoon, create a slight well in each meringue for the cream and berries.

6. Preheat the oven to 225°F.

7. Bake the meringues on the center rack for 30 minutes. Turn down the oven to 200°F and bake for another 60 minutes. You can bake the pavlovas one tray at a time on the middle rack of the oven, but if you prefer to bake them in one batch, place one on the top rack and one on the bottom rack and switch their positions when you lower the oven temperature to 200°F.

8. After 1½ hours, the meringues should be crispy on the outside and marshmallow-soft on the inside. If you can easily lift them up and hear a hollow sound when you tap the bottom, they are done. Bake them for another 5 minutes if they're not quite ready. When done, remove the pavlovas from the oven and let cool completely on the baking sheets.

9. While the meringues cool, prepare the cream. Using a handheld or stand mixer, whisk the cream, adding the icing sugar 1 tablespoon at a time. Add the vanilla, and continue beating until the cream is fully whipped and stiff peaks have formed.

10. Spoon cream into each cooled meringue. Add your choice of fruit and berries and enjoy.

Chocolate and Caramel Poke Cake

Poke cake is a classic that is always a welcome sight to anyone coming in off the trail. It has been a part of the backcountry afternoon tea service for as long as anyone I know can remember. This version takes a simple, moist chocolate cake recipe and kicks it up a notch with a few pokes of calorie-replenishing caramel and an icing that I can only describe as decadent.

SERVES 12

Here's what you'll need:

CAKE:

⅔ cup cocoa powder, plus extra for dusting

3 cups all-purpose flour

2 cups granulated sugar

2 teaspoons baking soda

1 teaspoon baking powder

1 teaspoon kosher salt

2 cups ice-cold water

½ cup canola oil

1 tablespoon lemon juice

1 teaspoon vanilla extract

CARAMEL POKE:

2 cups granulated sugar

1 (14 oz) can sweetened condensed milk

½ cup salted butter, divided

2 teaspoons vanilla extract

ICING:

2½ cups icing sugar

¾ cup cocoa powder

1 cup unsalted butter, at room temperature

Kosher salt

2 teaspoons vanilla extract

¼ cup whipping (35–40%) cream

½ cup chopped pecans (optional)

Here's how it's done:

1. Preheat the oven to 350°F. Grease a 13- × 9-inch baking dish. Dust lightly with cocoa powder and discard any extra.

2. To make the cake, in a large mixing bowl, whisk the flour with the cocoa and sugar. Add the baking soda, baking powder, and salt and whisk to combine. Using a heavy whisk, quickly add the water and oil to the dry ingredients. Whisk well to combine, about 1 to 2 minutes. Add the lemon juice and vanilla and whisk until the batter is smooth and shiny.

3. Pour the batter into the prepared baking dish and bake for 50 to 60 minutes, or until a cake tester inserted into the center of the cake comes out clean.

4. While the cake is in the oven, prepare the caramel poke and icing. In a heavy-bottomed saucepan over medium-high heat, combine the sugar with ½ cup of water. Cook, whisking continuously, until the sugar dissolves. Turn down the heat to low and allow the sugar water to simmer, untouched, for 10 to 12 minutes, or until it turns a gorgeous caramel color and has begun to thicken. Do not allow the kids to stick their fingers in the pan. It's tempting, but hot sugar is not to be messed with.

5. Remove the caramel from the heat to cool for a couple of minutes and then slowly pour in the condensed milk. It could boil over, so going slowly is key. Whisk well to combine and then add about 2 tablespoons of the butter, whisking continuously to help it melt. Add the rest of the butter and the vanilla in a single addition. Turn the heat back on low and mix gently to melt and combine. Set aside once you have achieved a smooth and silky texture with a warm caramel color.

6. Remove the cake from the oven and let cool in the pan on a wire rack.

7. Once it has cooled, use the handle of a wooden spoon to make deep pokes in the top of the cake. I usually do five widthwise and eight to ten lengthwise. Pour the caramel sauce over top of the entire cake and into all the holes. (Remember to reserve some if you want to put any on the iced top.)

8. To make the icing, sift the icing sugar and cocoa powder together into a mixing bowl. Use a handheld or stand mixer to beat the butter until smooth and lump free. Add the sifted icing sugar and cocoa and beat on medium speed until smooth and slightly fluffy. Add a pinch of salt, followed by the vanilla. Turn the mixer speed to low and slowly pour in the heavy cream until blended. Set the speed back to medium and blend until icing is smooth and spreadable.

9. Ice the cake with an offset spatula or icing palette. If you've saved some caramel, drizzle it over the icing and sprinkle the chopped pecans (if using) overtop.

Beet Hummus

Hummus has been a go-to snack of mine for a long time. You can pair it with chips, crackers, veggies, your finger, anything really. This version has a gorgeous, earthy color from the beets, as well as the glorious texture of a traditional hummus. When you pair this with the crispy fun of a zigadenus cracker (page 60), you get perfection!

MAKES 2 CUPS

Here's what you'll need:

2 small beets

2 tablespoons extra virgin olive oil,
   plus extra for drizzling

1 bulb garlic

1½ cups chickpeas, drained and rinsed

2 tablespoons tahini

3 tablespoons lemon juice

3–4 tablespoons cold water

½ teaspoon ground cumin

½ teaspoon ground coriander

Kosher salt and ground black pepper

Here's how it's done:

1. Preheat the oven to 375°F.

2. Place the beets on a large sheet of aluminum foil and drizzle with a bit of oil. Lightly peel the outer layers of skin from the garlic bulb and cut ¼ inch off the top to expose the cloves. Place the garlic bulb on the foil with the beets, drizzle with a bit more oil, and close up the foil package.

3. Place the foil package in a small baking dish and roast for 40 to 60 minutes, until the beets are fork-tender.

4. Once cool, discard the skin of the beets and chop the beets into bite-size pieces. Place the beets in a food processor and pulse for 1 minute. Squeeze out four to five cloves of the roasted garlic and add them to the food processor, along with the chickpeas and tahini. Turn the food processor on, and while it's running, drizzle in the 2 tablespoons of olive oil and the lemon juice. Add the water, 1 tablespoon at a time, until you get the desired consistency. Mix in the cumin, coriander, and salt and pepper to taste and pulse to combine. Add more water if it looks too thick. Taste the hummus, and add more lemon, olive oil, or salt to taste.

5. Hummus will keep in the fridge for up to 5 days, though it's best if consumed within 3.

Zigadenus Crackers

I used to be so intimidated at the thought of making my own crackers. I figured I'd never be able to even come close to those in the grocery store. But I was wrong! Named after a stunning glacier-fed lake in Banff National Park, this recipe combines crunch with style, and it's easier to make than you might expect.

MAKES ABOUT 4 DOZEN CRACKERS

Here's what you'll need:

2 cups all-purpose flour

2 teaspoons baking soda

1 teaspoon kosher salt

¼ cup demerara sugar

2 cups buttermilk

¼ cup maple syrup

½ cup dried cherries

½ cup dried chopped figs or apricots

½ cup roasted pumpkin seeds

3 tablespoons roasted sunflower seeds

1 tablespoon black sesame seeds

2 teaspoons flax seeds

3 tablespoons grated Parmigiano-Reggiano cheese

1 tablespoon chopped fresh rosemary leaves

1 tablespoon chopped fresh chives

Here's how it's done:

1. Preheat the oven to 350°F. Grease two 9- × 5-inch loaf pans. Line the bottom of each pan with parchment paper. Press it in with your fingers to make sure it is snug.

2. In a large mixing bowl or the bowl of a stand mixer, use a spatula or wooden spoon to mix together the flour, baking soda, and salt. Add the demerara sugar, making sure there are no lumps in it. Add the buttermilk and use a handheld mixer or the stand mixer to mix well. Mix in the maple syrup.

3. With the machine running on low, mix in the dried fruits and all the seeds. Scrape down the sides and bottom of the bowl.

4. Mix in the cheese, rosemary, and chives.

5. Turn the dough over a couple of times with a sturdy spatula and divide the mixture between the prepared loaf pans. Shimmy the loaf pans slightly to ensure the dough is lying flat and the mixture is poured evenly.

6. Bake on the middle rack of the oven for 30 to 35 minutes, or until the dough springs back when touched. Cool in the pans for a couple of minutes and then remove from the pans and transfer to a wire rack to cool completely.

7. Wrap in plastic wrap and refrigerate for at least 5 hours, but preferably overnight.

8. Preheat the oven to 350°F. Line two baking sheets with parchment paper.

9. Remove the loaves from the fridge, peel off and discard the parchment, and cut the loaves into thin cracker-like slices. You should get between 23 and 25 crackers from each loaf.

10. Place the crackers on the baking sheet, leaving enough room between them to let you turn them over easily. You may need to do this in batches.

11. Bake one tray at a time on the center rack of the oven for 20 minutes, turning 180 degrees halfway through baking time. (If you're baking both trays at once, place one on the top rack and one on the bottom rack and swap their positions halfway through baking time, when you rotate them.)

12. Let cool on the baking tray and voilà! You've got some awesome crackers for your hummus (page 59).

13. These can be stored in the fridge in an airtight container for up to 1 week or the freezer for up to 1 month.

Delightfully Cheesy Crisps

I started making these crackers to pack in my children's lunch boxes as an alternative to store-bought snacks, which often contain nuts. They are now a staple around our place, and I'm sure they will grow into a family favorite at your place too.

MAKES ABOUT 1½ DOZEN CRACKERS

Here's what you'll need:

1 cup salted butter, softened

1 (8 oz) package sharp, cold-packed cheddar spread (I use MacLaren's Imperial)

¼ teaspoon hot sauce

¼ teaspoon Worcestershire sauce

¼ teaspoon garlic powder

Coarse kosher salt

4 cups crispy rice cereal

1½ cups all-purpose flour

Here's how it's done:

1. Preheat the oven to 350°F. Line two baking sheets with parchment paper.

2. Using a handheld or stand mixer, beat the butter with the cheese spread. You are looking for a thick and creamy texture. You might have to scrape down the sides of the bowl a couple of times before you reach the right consistency.

3. Add the hot sauce, Worcestershire, garlic powder, and a pinch of salt and mix well to combine.

4. With the mixer running on low speed, add 1 cup of the rice cereal, followed by ½ cup of the flour, alternating in this way until you've added all the flour and cereal. Continue mixing until the ingredients are well incorporated. The dough should feel a bit sticky.

5. Spoon the dough into balls using a tablespoon measure and place them on the prepared baking sheets, 1 inch apart. Press down with the back of a fork to create a crisscross pattern. You might need some cold water on standby to dip the fork in, so it doesn't stick.

6. Bake one tray at a time on the center rack of the oven for 13 to 16 minutes, or until the edges are golden and the crackers are crispy. (If you're baking both trays at once, place one on the top rack and one on the bottom rack and swap their positions halfway through baking time.)

7. Using a spatula, transfer the crackers to a wire rack to cool completely.

8. You can store these in an airtight container or resealable bag at room temperature for up to 1 week.

Rice Wraps with Marinated Chicken and Peanut Dipping Sauce

These make a terrific lunch or a great afternoon tea goodie with a round of backgammon on a stormy day. You can always swap out the rice paper wraps for lettuce and use any vegetables you prefer. The chicken can also easily be substituted with tofu or beans for a vegetarian option. Do not be tempted to swap out the marinade or dipping sauce!

SERVES 6

Here's what you'll need:

CHICKEN:

⅓ cup vegetable stock

3 tablespoons soy sauce

1 tablespoon rice vinegar

2 teaspoons sambal oelek

1½-inch piece ginger, peeled and chopped

1 garlic clove, minced

2 teaspoons granulated sugar

2 medium boneless, skinless chicken breasts, pan-fried and cut into strips lengthwise

DIPPING SAUCE:

¾ cup smooth peanut butter

2 tablespoons hoisin sauce

5 teaspoons soy sauce

1½ tablespoons lime juice

2 teaspoons sriracha

1 teaspoon sesame oil

2 cloves garlic, crushed

1 tablespoon granulated sugar

WRAPS:

12 rice paper wraps (see note)

1 cup cooked basmati rice

1 cup julienned carrot

6 radishes, julienned

1 yellow bell pepper, julienned

2 green onions, thinly chopped

½ cup roughly chopped cilantro

⅓ cup chopped roasted salted peanuts

Here's how it's done:

1. Let's begin with the marinade so it is ready to rock and roll when you are. In a mixing bowl, whisk the stock, soy sauce, rice vinegar, and sambal oelek with the ginger, garlic, and sugar. Add the cooked chicken. Stir to coat the chicken evenly and refrigerate, covered, for at least 3 hours, or up to overnight.

2. Remove the chicken breasts from the marinade, shaking off any excess and discarding the marinade.

3. To make the dipping sauce, in a mixing bowl, whisk the peanut butter with the hoisin and soy sauces until the mixture is smooth. Add ⅓ cup water, the lime juice, sriracha, sesame oil, garlic, and sugar. Mix until sauce reaches your desired thickness, then set aside.

4. To prepare the wraps, place 1½ to 2 cups of very warm water in a shallow bowl. One at a time, lay the rice paper sheets in the water for 30 seconds, turn over and soak for 10 seconds, then lift out and let any excess water drip off. Lay the softened rice paper sheets on a clean work surface or plate and place some cooked rice, carrots, radishes, bell pepper, green onions, cilantro, and peanuts in the center of each sheet, making sure they don't poke through the ends of the rice paper. Place a couple of strips of marinated chicken breast over the vegetables.

5. Roll up the rice paper wraps by first folding one half toward the middle and folding the other half over to meet it. Starting at one of the open edges, roll the wrap up tightly but carefully, so as not to tear the paper. Place on a dry platter when finished rolling. You will most likely need to wipe the table dry a few times, but you don't need to be too fussy.

6. Serve the peanut dipping sauce in individual bowls, because we all know we'll double-dip!

NOTE: I prefer to use rice paper made with tapioca, as it seems to hold up better and doesn't crumple up as easily in the water as do non-tapioca papers. This recipe can be doubled or tripled for a wonderful party tray or buffet staple.

Timberland Pizza

You will never see happier faces than when you pull this pizza out of the oven in front of a crowd of skiers. Seriously, the wonderful, freshly baked pizza aroma gets the lodge guests out of their ski boots faster than fresh snow gets them out on the hill. (Note that you might prefer to prep this the night before you plan to eat it.)

SERVES 6–8

Here's what you'll need:

RED SAUCE:

1 (28 oz) can crushed tomatoes

2 garlic cloves, crushed

2 tablespoons extra virgin olive oil

1½ teaspoons kosher salt

1 teaspoon dried oregano

½ teaspoon dried basil

DOUGH:

2 cups all-purpose flour

1½ teaspoons instant yeast

1 teaspoon kosher salt

1 teaspoon dried thyme leaves

¾ cup tap-hot water

2 teaspoons extra virgin olive oil, plus extra for the baking sheet

4 tablespoons cornmeal

TOPPINGS:

1 tablespoon extra virgin olive oil

1 red onion, thinly sliced

1 yellow bell pepper, cut into ¼-inch strips

1 fennel bulb, end removed, thinly sliced

3–4 garlic cloves, roasted (see note)

1½ cups shredded mozzarella

1½ cups fresh mozzarella, sliced into rounds

Here's how it's done:

1. I like to make the red sauce a good 24 hours in advance so that the seasonings can mingle and the flavor profile can develop. In a large saucepan over low heat, mix together the tomatoes, garlic, oil, salt, oregano, and basil. Bring to a simmer, stirring occasionally and cook, uncovered, for 1 hour, or until the sauce thickens. Remove from the heat and allow to cool for 20 to 30 minutes before puréeing. Using a blender or an immersion blender, purée until smooth. If using an immersion blender, make sure you are wearing an apron. You are looking for a sauce thick enough to coat the back of a wooden spoon. If the consistency is still too thin, return it to the saucepan and cook for another 15 minutes. Let cool, then cover and refrigerate. Remove the sauce from the fridge about 30 minutes prior to starting the pizza assembly (Step 10), draining off any excess liquid.

2. To make the dough, in a large bowl, mix the flour, yeast, salt, and thyme with the water and oil. Using your hands, knead the dough until it forms a ball.

3. Turn the dough out onto a lightly floured work surface. Using both hands, knead the dough: Press the center of the dough with the heels of your hands, then push them onto the dough and away from you. Using quarter turns, pull the dough back toward you with the heels of your hands, adding only enough flour to keep the dough from sticking. Continue this process until you begin to feel air developing in the dough and it is smooth and springs back when poked with your finger. This whole process should take between 6 and 8 minutes.

4. Lightly oil a large mixing bowl, place the dough in it, turning once to ensure the whole ball is covered with oil, and cover with a tea towel. Set aside in a warm, draft-free spot to rise for up to 1 hour, or until doubled in size.

5. Preheat the oven to 450°F.

6. After the dough has risen, gently punch it down in bowl, then turn it out onto a lightly floured surface, and, dusting the rolling pin lightly with flour if necessary, roll out the dough to fit a large baking sheet or pizza stone. If you're using a half sheet pan, you'll need to divide the dough in two.

7. Grease the baking sheet with a generous amount of olive oil to coat the tray (there's no need to grease a pizza stone, if that's what you're using). Sprinkle the cornmeal overtop. Place the rolled-out dough on the baking sheet and shimmy it into position, pushing the dough into the corners gently to avoid tearing it. Bake the crust for 10 minutes. Remove from the oven and use a spatula to lift the crust immediately to avoid any sticking. Keep the oven switched on.

8. To make the toppings, in a cast iron skillet over medium-high heat, warm the oil. Sauté the onion, bell pepper, and fennel until just beginning to soften, about 5 minutes.

9. Squeeze the roasted garlic over the vegetables. Remove the skillet from the heat and set aside.

10. Spread the red sauce over the pizza dough. Distribute the vegetables evenly overtop. Sprinkle the shredded mozzarella over the whole pizza and arrange the fresh mozzarella in neat rows.

11. Bake for 8 to 12 minutes, or until the crust is golden and crispy and the cheese is completely melted and bubbly.

NOTE: To roast the garlic, preheat the oven to 375°F. Peel any papery outer layers off the bulb. Cut ¼ inch of the head off the garlic to expose the individual cloves. Drizzle the entire bulb with olive oil and wrap up in aluminum foil. Roast directly on the middle oven rack for 35 to 40 minutes. Remove from the oven and unwrap the garlic. Once it's cooled, you can separate individual cloves from the bulb to squeeze.

Purcell Mountain Lodge

The flight from Golden, BC, into Purcell Mountain Lodge is an amazing introduction to what is to come: tumbling glaciers, breathtaking peaks, meadows upon meadows of gorgeous hiking trails with knee-deep wildflowers, and opportunities to see boundless wildlife, all leading to a three-story stunner of a lodge. Then, when you enter, you are greeted with its famous hospitality, a roaring fire, and mouthwatering meals to delight everyone.

The true spirit of the lodge is brought to life by a colorful cast of characters—the hosts, caretakers, and guides—who are all enthusiastic about the day-to-day life at the lodge and doing what they love outdoors, whether that be skiing, hiking, snowshoeing, biking, or meditating under the watchful slopes of Bald Mountain.

After a day spent exploring the classic backcountry terrain of the Northern Purcell Mountains, the lodge team and guests often find themselves back around a well-loved harvest table. This is where meals are shared, summit objectives are mapped, and stories flow like wine between folks who might have come as strangers but leave as friends. The table's polished wood has been smoothed out over the years, not just by countless mugs of tea but also by the moments and memories of three decades of backcountry living at its best.

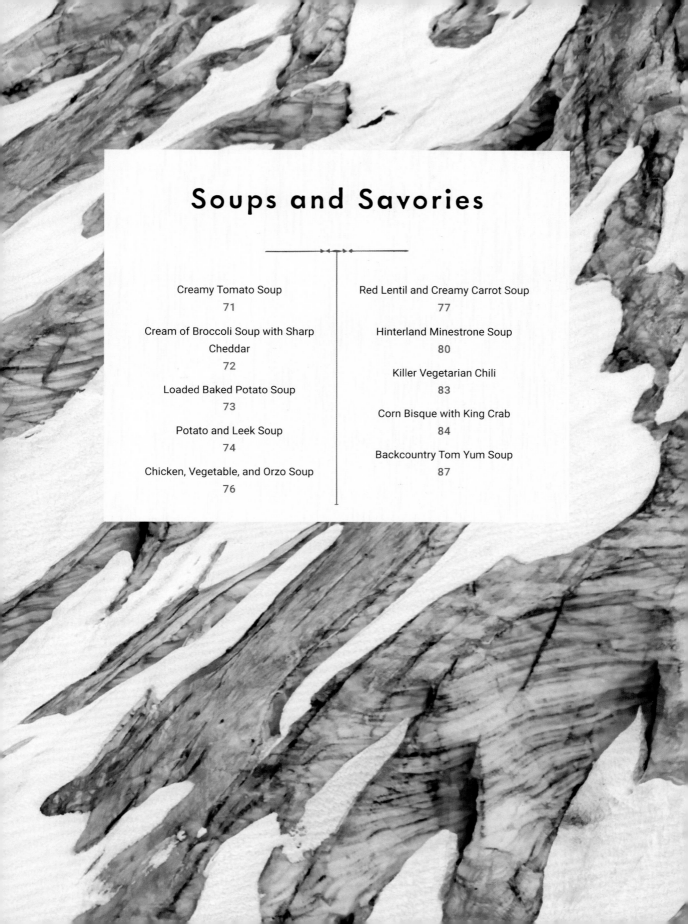

Soups and Savories

Creamy Tomato Soup

When the air turns crisp, the craving for warming soups is tough to ignore. This creamy tomato soup offers a soothing balance of acidity and rich creaminess—and the perfect welcome home after a day of walking among the fall larches.

SERVES 6–8

Here's what you'll need:

2 tablespoons salted butter

1 tablespoon extra virgin olive oil

1 medium white onion, diced

3 garlic cloves, crushed

2 (each 28 oz) cans peeled whole tomatoes

1 (6 oz) can tomato paste

4 cups vegetable stock

2 tablespoons lemon juice

Kosher salt and ground black pepper

Hot sauce (optional)

2 cups whipping (35–40%) cream

Handful of fresh flat-leaf or curly parsley, finely chopped (optional)

Here's how it's done:

1. In a large, heavy-bottomed soup pot or Dutch oven over medium heat, melt the butter with the olive oil. Add the onion and garlic and sauté for about 5 to 6 minutes, or until the onion starts to soften and become translucent.

2. Transfer the onion and garlic to a blender, add the tomatoes in batches, purée, and then add the mixture to the pot along with the tomato paste. Whisk to incorporate well.

3. Add the stock and lemon juice and bring to a simmer. Add salt and pepper to taste and a splash of hot sauce (if using).

4. Simmer, uncovered, for about 20 minutes, or until the soup starts to thicken. Add the cream and stir well. (You might prefer to use more than 2 cups of cream in this.) Finish with black pepper or the parsley.

Cream of Broccoli Soup with Sharp Cheddar

Many people don't think of soup in the summer, but I find that lodge guests can eat a lot of broccoli and cheddar soup even on the hottest of days. It offers nourishment and energy to their calorie-depleted bodies after a day of hiking, and it can also bring out a round of smiles among the weary new arrivals, who weren't expecting such a wonderful welcome.

SERVES 4–6

Here's what you'll need:

6 tablespoons salted butter

1 white onion, chopped

2 garlic cloves, crushed

¼ cup all-purpose flour

2½ cups 2% milk

4 cups chicken stock

½ teaspoon ground nutmeg

½ teaspoon ground cardamom

Kosher salt and ground black pepper

4 cups broccoli florets

1½–2 cups whipping (35–40%) cream

2½ cups grated sharp, aged cheddar cheese

Thyme sprigs, for garnish

Here's how it's done:

1. In a large, heavy-bottomed soup pot or Dutch oven over medium heat, melt the butter. Add the onion and garlic and sauté for 5 to 6 minutes, or until the onion starts to soften and become translucent. Stir in the flour and cook, still stirring, for a couple of minutes, making sure the flour doesn't brown. Whisk in the milk until the mixture is smooth. It is important to take your time to incorporate all the flour into the milk, so you aren't left with any lumps.

2. Whisk in the stock 1 cup at a time, whisking well between additions. Add the nutmeg, cardamom, and salt and pepper to taste, and whisk to combine. Turn the heat down to low and simmer, uncovered, for about 20 minutes.

3. Add the broccoli florets and continue to heat on a low simmer for another 20 minutes. (Some people prefer to steam the broccoli before adding it to the broth, but I like the taste when it cooks in the stock instead.)

4. Remove from the heat and let cool for 20 to 30 minutes before puréeing. If you are using a food processor or blender, do so in batches. If using an immersion blender, make sure you are wearing an apron.

5. Return the soup to the pot, add the cream, and place the pot over medium-low heat to gently warm the soup. If the soup is too thick for your liking, add more stock or cream. You can even add hot water if you prefer less richness.

6. Turn up the heat to medium, and add the cheese a handful at a time. Whisk until the cheese has melted and is incorporated into the soup.

7. This soup is a stunner served with a thyme sprig.

Loaded Baked Potato Soup

Who doesn't love a baked potato? The butter, sour cream, bacon bits, and chives, and the tender flesh of a perfectly cooked potato—oh my goodness. This recipe has all the usual suspects and a few more. It eats like a meal and can be paired with a salad and flatbread to take it to the next level.

SERVES 6

Here's what you'll need:

3 tablespoons extra virgin olive oil, divided

1 medium white onion, diced

2 garlic cloves, crushed

2 celery stalks, chopped

2 chicken bouillon cubes, crushed

2 lb russet potatoes, peeled and cubed

1 teaspoon granulated sugar

1 teaspoon kosher salt

1 teaspoon ground black pepper

1 teaspoon paprika (any type)

½ teaspoon garlic powder

½ teaspoon onion powder

6 cups chicken stock

6 tablespoons salted butter

1 (8 oz) package cream cheese, cubed

¾ cup 2% milk

½ cup whipping (35–40%) cream

8 slices bacon, cooked and crumbled

1 cup full-fat sour cream

½ cup chopped fresh chives

Here's how it's done:

1. In a large, heavy-bottomed soup pot or Dutch oven over medium heat, warm 2 tablespoons of oil. Add the onion, garlic, celery, and bouillon cubes and cook for 5 to 6 minutes, until the onion starts to soften and become translucent. Add the potatoes and the remaining 1 tablespoon oil. Mix to combine, cover the pan, and cook for about 10 more minutes, stirring occasionally.

2. Mix in the sugar, salt, pepper, paprika, garlic powder, and onion powder.

3. Add 6 cups of the stock, turn up the heat to medium-high, and bring to a rolling boil. Boil, uncovered, for 8 to 10 minutes and then turn down the heat to low. Simmer for 20 minutes.

4. Remove from the heat and let cool for 20 to 30 minutes before puréeing. If you are using a food processor or blender, do so in batches. If using an immersion blender, make sure you are wearing an apron.

5. Return the soup to the pot.

6. In a small saucepan over low heat, melt the butter. Add the cream cheese, a few pieces at a time, and slowly melt until smooth, about 10 minutes. Add the milk and whisk to combine. Bring to a simmer and cook for another 5 minutes.

7. Pour the cream cheese mixture into the soup pot along with the cream. Add the bacon and stir to combine.

8. Serve hot with a dollop of sour cream and a generous sprinkle of chives.

Potato and Leek Soup

This classic recipe is a wonderfully warm and inviting soup. It can be served as the main course or as an afternoon treat after a fun day of birdwatching outdoors. The seasonings and fresh herbs make it an eye-catching and aromatic dish.

SERVES 8–10

Here's what you'll need:

2 tablespoons salted butter

1 tablespoon vegetable oil

4 leeks, washed and chopped

4 garlic cloves, crushed

2 lb russet potatoes, peeled and cubed

8 cups vegetable or chicken stock

2 bay leaves

1 teaspoon fresh dill leaves

1 teaspoon fresh thyme leaves

Kosher salt and ground black pepper

2 cups whipping (35–40%) cream

Handful fresh flat-leaf or curly parsley, chopped

Greek yogurt (optional)

Thyme sprigs (optional)

Here's how it's done:

1. In a large, heavy-bottomed soup pot or Dutch oven over medium heat, melt the butter with the oil. Add the leeks and garlic and sauté for about 10 minutes, or until the leeks start to soften and become translucent.

2. Add the potatoes and stock. Turn up the heat to medium-high. Add the bay leaves, thyme, dill, and salt and pepper to taste and mix to combine. Bring to a gentle boil and keep it there for about 5 minutes. Turn down the temperature to low and simmer, uncovered, for about 20 to 30 minutes, or until the potatoes are fork-tender.

3. Remove from the heat and let cool for 20 to 30 minutes. Remove the bay leaves and purée the soup. If you are using a food processor or blender, do so in batches. If using an immersion blender, make sure you are wearing an apron.

4. Return the soup to the pot, add the cream, and place the pot over medium-low heat to gently warm the soup. Add in the fresh parsley, stirring to combine.

5. Garnish with a dollop of Greek yogurt (if using) and some thyme sprigs (if using).

Chicken, Vegetable, and Orzo Soup

The wonderful aromas of this soup will draw people to the kitchen. Its hearty ingredients make it a great choice to share with family and friends after a fall day of kicking leaves and working up an appetite in the cool air.

SERVES 6–8

Here's what you'll need:

3 tablespoons salted butter, plus extra for serving

2 tablespoons extra virgin olive oil

1 large white onion, diced

3 garlic cloves, minced

1½ cups peeled and cubed butternut squash

2 carrots, chopped

2 celery stalks, chopped

1 leek, washed and chopped

1 turnip, peeled and diced

1 fennel bulb, ends off, peeled, thinly sliced

6 Brussels sprouts, ends off, quartered

8 cups chicken stock, divided

2 boneless, skinless chicken breasts, cooked and shredded

½ cup frozen peas

½ cup frozen corn kernels

⅓ cup quartered yellow beans

Kosher salt and ground black pepper

1 cup cooked orzo

3 green onions, chopped

8 fresh mint leaves, chopped

1 tablespoon fresh thyme leaves

French baguette, warmed, for serving

Here's how it's done:

1. In a large, heavy-bottomed soup pot or Dutch oven over medium heat, melt the butter with the oil. Add the onion and garlic and sauté for 5 to 6 minutes, or until the onion starts to soften and become translucent. Add the squash, carrot, celery, leek, turnip, fennel, and Brussels sprouts. Stir gently to combine. Continue to sauté for an additional 10 to 12 minutes, or until all the vegetables are fork-tender and sweetly aromatic.

2. Pour in 2 cups of the stock and cover the pan. Cook for about 10 minutes, stirring occasionally. Add the chicken, peas, corn, and beans. Stir to combine with the other ingredients and then add the remaining 6 cups of stock and salt and pepper to taste.

3. Return to the heat, bring to a simmer, and cook, covered, for 20 to 25 minutes, or until all the vegetables are tender. Add the orzo and stir it into the soup to warm through.

4. Stir in the green onion, mint, and thyme. Serve immediately with a warm baguette smothered in butter.

Red Lentil and Creamy Carrot Soup

Sometimes I feel like I use a lot of rich ingredients in my soups. Does it seem that way to you too? No bother, we are hikers and skiers—aka hungry people. There is not a journey we can't take that won't crush those calories, so grab your walking shoes and stroll to the market for the ingredients for this delightful soup. But, surprise! You won't need any cream. The creaminess comes from the purée and the coconut milk.

SERVES 6–8

Here's what you'll need:

1 tablespoon salted butter

1 tablespoon extra virgin olive oil

2 medium white onions, diced

2 garlic cloves, minced

4 carrots, roughly chopped

1-inch piece ginger, peeled and minced

1 teaspoon granulated sugar

1 teaspoon ground coriander

1 teaspoon ground cumin

½ teaspoon ground turmeric

Kosher salt and ground black pepper

6 cups chicken stock, divided

¾ cups dried red lentils

1 (13.5 oz) can coconut milk

1 carrot, grated

½ cup freshly chopped cilantro, or more to taste

Here's how it's done:

1. In a large, heavy-bottomed soup pot or Dutch oven over medium heat, melt the butter with the oil. Add the onion and garlic and sauté for 5 to 6 minutes, or until the onion starts to soften and become translucent. Add the carrots, ginger, sugar, coriander, cumin, turmeric, and a large pinch each of salt and pepper. Mix to combine.

2. Pour in 1 cup of the stock, bring to a simmer, and cook, uncovered, for 5 minutes.

3. Rinse the lentils in a colander and set aside.

4. Add the remaining 5 cups of stock and turn up the heat to medium-high. Add the lentils, stir, and bring to a boil. Boil for a full minute and then turn down the heat to a low simmer. Simmer, uncovered, for 20 to 25 minutes.

5. Remove from the heat and let cool for 20 to 30 minutes before puréeing. If you are using a food processor or blender, do so in batches. If using an immersion blender, make sure you are wearing an apron.

6. Return the soup to the pot, add the coconut milk, and place the pot over medium-low heat. Bring back to a low simmer until warmed through. Garnish with a sprinkle of grated carrot and chopped cilantro.

Hinterland Minestrone Soup

Canadian winters are marked by the number of days we crave hot soup. Inspired by the classic Italian dish, this hinterland minestrone soup offers all of the savory flavors you crave on a cold day. It's a fitting soup to take along in your thermos for an afternoon of outdoor skating on a frozen pond.

SERVES 5–6

Here's what you'll need:

2 tablespoons vegetable oil

1 medium white onion, chopped

4 garlic cloves, minced

3 celery stalks, chopped

3 carrots, chopped

½ cup diced green or yellow beans

1 (28 oz) can whole plum tomatoes

1 (14.5 oz) can fire roasted diced tomatoes

1 (15.5 oz) can kidney beans, drained and rinsed

6 cups chicken stock

1 teaspoon dried oregano

1 teaspoon dried basil

1 teaspoon dried thyme leaves

¼ teaspoon dried marjoram

Kosher salt and ground black pepper

1½ cups tortellini or farfalle pasta

Freshly grated Parmigiano-Reggiano cheese, for garnish

Fresh basil leaves, chiffonade, for garnish

Here's how it's done:

1. In a large, heavy-bottomed soup pot or Dutch oven over medium heat, warm the oil. Add the onion and garlic and sauté for 5 to 6 minutes, or until the onion starts to soften and become translucent. Add the celery, carrots, and beans, mix to combine, and cook, covered, for another 5 minutes.

2. Pour the plum tomatoes and their juice into a bowl and crush them with your hands, removing any stems. Add the tomatoes and their juices to the pot, followed by the diced tomatoes and their juices and the kidney beans. Now add the stock, stirring to combine and lifting anything that may have lodged itself on the bottom of the pot.

3. Add the oregano, basil, thyme, marjoram, and salt and pepper to taste. Mix well. Bring to a simmer and cook, uncovered, for 2 to 3 minutes and then add the pasta. Cook the pasta in the soup for 10 to 12 minutes.

4. Garnish with a generous helping of Parmigiano-Reggiano and basil.

NOTE: If you don't intend to eat all of the soup in one sitting, you can cook the pasta separately and add it to the soup in individual portions as needed.

Killer Vegetarian Chili

Chili is a welcome sight on any occasion. With this killer chili recipe, it's hard to stop at just one serving, no matter what you've been up to. The array of vegetables, beans, and seasonings will have everyone hoping for a little bit more of this delicious one-pot meal.

SERVES 6–8

Here's what you'll need:

2 tablespoons vegetable oil

1 large white onion, chopped

4 garlic cloves, minced

2 celery stalks, chopped

2 carrots, chopped

2 cups sliced button mushrooms

1 red bell pepper, chopped

1 yellow bell pepper, chopped

2 jalapeño peppers, seeded and chopped

1 cup vegetable stock

2 tablespoons white wine vinegar

1 tablespoon smooth Dijon mustard

¼ cup ketchup

2 (each 28 oz) cans whole plum tomatoes

1 (14.5 oz) can diced tomatoes

1 (15.5 oz) can kidney beans, drained and rinsed

1 (15.5 oz) can black beans, drained and rinsed

1 (15.5 oz) can chickpeas, drained and rinsed

2–3 tablespoons brown sugar

2 tablespoons molasses

¼ cup chili powder

1 teaspoon ground cinnamon

1 teaspoon ground cumin

1 teaspoon dried thyme leaves

3 tablespoons sriracha or your favorite hot sauce (optional)

Sour cream and grated Parmigiano-Reggiano cheese, for serving

Here's how it's done:

1. In a large, heavy-bottomed soup pot or Dutch oven over medium heat, warm the oil. Add the onion, garlic, celery, and carrots and mix to combine. Sweat the vegetables for 5 to 6 minutes, or until the onion starts to become translucent and the carrots are still al dente. Add the mushrooms, bell and jalapeño peppers, and then the stock. Continue to cook on medium heat for 8 minutes and then stir in the vinegar and Dijon, followed by the ketchup.

2. Pour the plum tomatoes and their juice into a bowl and crush them with your hands, removing any stems. Add the tomatoes and their juices to the pot, followed by the diced tomatoes and their juices. Add the beans and chickpeas.

3. Stir in the brown sugar (to taste) and molasses, followed by the chili powder, cinnamon, cumin, thyme, and sriracha or your favorite hot sauce (the hot sauce is completely optional, but this is called "killer chili" for a reason, so I say go for it).

4. Using a wooden spoon or long-handled spatula, get up underneath the chili and mix all the ingredients.

5. Turn down the heat to low, bring to a simmer, and cook, uncovered, for 30 to 40 minutes. Taste for seasonings. Add more brown sugar or molasses to cut down the acidity of the tomatoes, or a pinch more cinnamon to enhance the deep flavor profile and develop the aromatics. Whatever you decide, this will be perfect served with a dollop of sour cream and some freshly grated Parmigiano-Reggiano.

Corn Bisque with King Crab

Storm watching is a favorite activity for many folks who would rather be inside a warm building with their backs to the fire than outside leaning into the wind. This hearty soup is a wonderful dish for such an occasion.

SERVES 6

Here's what you'll need:

½ cup salted butter

1 medium white onion, diced

1 leek, washed and thinly sliced

3 garlic cloves, minced

3 tablespoons all-purpose flour

2 cups 2% milk

1 tablespoon white wine vinegar

1½ lb red potatoes, scrubbed and cubed

2 jalapeño peppers, seeded and diced

1 red bell pepper, diced

6 cups chicken stock

1 tablespoon garlic powder

1 tablespoon onion powder

2 teaspoons dried thyme leaves

2 teaspoons paprika (any type)

1 teaspoon cayenne pepper

1 teaspoon dried oregano

2 cups roasted corn kernels

1 lb cooked crabmeat, shredded

Kosher salt and cracked black pepper

2 cups whipping (35–40%) cream

¼ cup chopped cilantro

Baguette, for serving

6 crab claws, for serving (optional)

Here's how it's done:

1. In a large, heavy-bottomed soup pot or Dutch oven over medium heat, melt the butter. Add the onion, leek, and garlic and mix to combine. Sauté the vegetables for 5 minutes, stirring once or twice.

2. Turn down the heat to medium-low and add the flour, 1 tablespoon at a time, mixing well between additions. Pour in the milk, 1 cup at a time, whisking to incorporate between additions. The mixture should be smooth. Add the vinegar and stir to combine.

3. Add the potatoes and the jalapeño and bell peppers, followed by the stock, and stir to combine. Add the garlic powder, onion powder, thyme, paprika, cayenne, and oregano. Stir well, bring to a simmer, and cook, uncovered, for 30 minutes, or until it starts to thicken and give off a fragrant aroma.

4. Add the corn and crabmeat, making sure there is no shell in sight. Season to taste with salt and pepper. Add the cream and stir to really combine all the ingredients and their flavors. Add the cilantro and stir lightly.

5. Turn down the heat and simmer, uncovered, for another 15 to 20 minutes. Serve in warm bowls with chunks of baguette (and chilled Sauvignon Blanc, if you like). And if you really want to take your presentation up a notch, serve with a crab claw.

Backcountry Tom Yum Soup

When I was in Brisbane, Australia, I lived in a weathered, wooden Queenslander, not far from the waterfront. On humid evenings, my roommates and I would often wander down to the local Thai takeout restaurant and order a Tom Yum soup that was otherworldly. This place was family-run and so authentic that just placing your order at the window had your eyes watering from the fragrant spices in the air. I like to make it at backcountry lodges because it can transform a cold winter day into the warmest of eating experiences.

SERVES 6

Here's what you'll need:

4 cups chicken stock

3 stalks lemongrass

1-inch piece ginger, peeled and minced

4 garlic cloves, coarsely chopped

8 fresh kaffir lime leaves, torn (see note)

2 tablespoons salted butter

1 lb large prawns or shrimp, shells removed

2 tablespoons sambal oelek, plus extra for garnish (garnish optional)

2 cups sliced white mushrooms

2 Roma tomatoes, cut in wedges

1 medium white onion

6 tablespoons fish sauce

Ground black pepper

2 teaspoons granulated sugar

1 (13.5 oz) can coconut milk (optional)

8 limes, juiced

½ teaspoon red chilies, chopped (optional)

1 bunch cilantro, chopped

Here's how it's done:

1. In a large, heavy-bottomed soup pot or Dutch oven over high heat, bring the stock and 4 cups of water to a boil.

2. Remove the outer leaves of the lemongrass and then roll it with a heavy rolling pin or hit it with a mallet to bruise it slightly. Chop on the bias into pieces about 2 inches long, and add to the boiling stock.

3. Add the ginger, garlic, and kaffir lime leaves and mix to combine. Turn down the heat to medium-high and lightly simmer, covered, for about 10 minutes.

4. Meanwhile, in a skillet over medium heat, melt the butter. Add the prawns and sauté for a couple of minutes before mixing in the sambal oelek. Fry the prawns for another full minute—they should still be somewhat gray—and then add them to the soup, along with any drippings from the pan. The prawns will continue to cook in the soup; they will become pink on the outside and opaque in the center.

5. Add the mushrooms to the broth and turn down the heat to medium-low. Cover the pot and allow the mushrooms to soften, about 8 to 10 minutes.

6. Add the tomatoes. Cut through the onion lengthwise, leaving the root end intact. Now cut through the root to make ½-inch wedges. This cut will ensure the wedges stay somewhat together. Stir the onion into the soup.

7. Add the fish sauce, and a pinch of pepper. Stir in the sugar, 1 teaspoon at a time, to taste. Stir in the coconut milk to combine. Continue to heat on medium-low for 5 more minutes.

8. Remove the soup from the heat and let cool for 10 minutes. If you want a creamier, more mild soup, serve as is. Otherwise, continue to the next step.

9. Add the lime juice a little bit at a time, until you reach a sour taste you find desirable. I like this soup sour, but some people prefer to keep it a little lower key. Warm the soup over low heat.

10. If you want to up the spice of the soup, add additional sambal oelek or seedless, chopped red chilies. Garnish with cilantro.

NOTE: If you can't find kaffir lime leaves at your grocery store, you can use one large, dried bay leaf and the grated zest from two limes. Add the bay leaf and zest at the same time as you would the kaffir leaves in the recipe. Remove the bay leaf before you add the lime juice.

Battle Abbey Country Lodge

Battle Abbey is one of the most spectacular lodges I have ever had the honor to work at. Perhaps it's because the Abbey brings out the very best in its people, and the people, in turn, wax poetic about its incredible skiing, location, and otherworldly views. Being there, you sense a deep passion for skiing and an unwavering commitment to beautiful friendships that together form the shared vision for the lodge you see to this day.

The lodge is located in the Selkirk Mountains of British Columbia and is situated on a high alpine shoulder overlooking Butter's Creek, with a spectacular view of the Battle Range, vast wildlife, and peak tops ranging up to 10,500 feet. The lodge is only accessible by helicopter out of Golden, BC, and the flight path crosses over the Purcell Mountains and South Glacier National Park.

Just outside Battle Abbey's front door, you can ski on the Selkirk powder—that can easily exceed well over 10 feet. And during the summer, guests can access remote and pristine environments, whether it's the Via Ferrata climbing route, mountaineering peaks, alpine rock climbing, or hiking trails. In the late summer in particular, the high alpine meadows are pocketed with flowers, which makes for truly magical hiking.

I always look back fondly on my time at the Abbey, where I skied its gorgeous and riveting terrain, struggled with immense emotion as the sun rose over the glorious mountains, and sipped hot tea while the guests spoke of the outdoor playground with the sparkle from the snow still in their eyes.

Breads

Artisan Cabin Bread

This is a no-knead, no-fuss bread. It is also a terrific jumping-off bread for the beginner baker. The steps are simple and the bread delivers on both taste and structure. (Note that you need to start this recipe the night before you plan to bake it.)

MAKES 1 LOAF

Here's what you'll need:

3 cups all-purpose flour, plus extra for dusting

2 teaspoons sea salt

½ teaspoon instant yeast

1½ cups tap-hot water

1 egg, beaten + 1 teaspoon water, for egg wash

Here's how it's done:

1. In a mixing bowl, stir the flour, salt, and yeast with a wooden spoon. Pour in the hot water, ½ cup at a time, mixing well between additions with the wooden spoon. The dough should be shaggy in both appearance and texture. Scrape down the sides of the bowl with a spatula and turn the dough over to make sure there is no dry flour left in the bowl. It is important not to work this dough too much, or it will not turn out light and fluffy. Cover with plastic wrap and set aside in a draft-free spot to rise overnight. It will double in size.

2. The next day, 30 minutes before you plan to bake the bread, place a baking stone in the oven and preheat the oven to 450°F. If you don't have a baking stone, you can use an inverted baking tray.

3. Meanwhile, lightly flour your hands and manipulate the dough into a semi-structured ball, reincorporating any stuck dough strands from the bottom and the sides of the bowl. Turn it out onto a lightly floured work surface. It should be double its original size and a little bubbly.

4. Using your hands, shape it into a ball and form a seam on one side. This should take about 2 to 3 minutes.

5. Remove the baking stone from the oven and dust the surface with flour. Gently place the dough ball in the center with the seam side down. Brush the top of the loaf with the egg wash. Using a lame or very sharp knife, score the loaf about ¼ inch deep a few times on a slight angle to give the accumulated air bubbles somewhere to go.

6. Bake on the middle rack of the oven for 40 minutes, or until the loaf is a golden color, the internal temperature is 190°F, and the loaf sounds hollow when you tap the bottom of the pan. Remove from the pan and let cool on a wire rack.

Perfect Lodge Toast Bread

Most of the lodges I have worked at have had limited sources of power: micro-hydro, solar, or generator. These power sources are meant for lighting the lodge or keeping the fridge running. They aren't really meant for using toasters or other small appliances, so most kitchen people rely on old-fashioned wire toasters, the type that sits right on top of a propane burner. This bread is delicious when toasted that way and then smothered in butter and fresh preserves—of course, it is equally tasty made in a conventional toaster.

MAKES 2 (9- × 5-INCH) LOAVES

Here's what you'll need:

Granulated sugar

½ cup tap-hot water

3 teaspoons active dry yeast

2 eggs

2 cups buttermilk

3 tablespoons salted butter, melted

3 tablespoons liquid honey

2 teaspoons lemon juice

6¼ cups all-purpose flour, divided, plus extra for kneading

Kosher salt

1 egg, beaten + 1 teaspoon water, for egg wash

Here's how it's done:

1. In a small bowl, dissolve a pinch of sugar in the water. Sprinkle the yeast in, stir very gently, and then let the mixture sit for about 8 to 10 minutes. When the yeast is bubbly and frothy, it is ready.

2. In a large mixing bowl, beat the eggs. Add the buttermilk, butter, honey, and lemon juice and whisk to combine. Stir in 3 cups of the flour and a pinch of salt. Fold in the yeast mixture. Mix in another 3 cups of the flour, 1 cup at a time and incorporating well between additions. Using your hands, bring the dough together until you have a lumpy, shaggy dough with no dry spots of flour, about 2 minutes. If the dough is really sticky, add another ¼ cup or so of flour until you have a tacky but not overly sticky texture.

3. Turn the dough out onto a lightly floured work surface. Using both hands, knead the dough. Press the center of the dough with the heels of your hands, then push them onto the dough and away from you. Using quarter turns, pull the dough back toward you with the heels of your hands, adding only enough extra flour to keep the dough from sticking. Continue this process until you begin to feel air developing in the dough and it is smooth and slightly tacky and springs back when poked with your finger. This whole process should take between 8 and 10 minutes.

4. Lightly oil a large mixing bowl and lightly dust it with all-purpose flour. Place the dough in the bowl, turning once to ensure the whole ball is covered with flour, and cover with a tea towel. Set aside in a warm, draft-free spot to rise for up to 1 hour, or until doubled in size.

5. Grease two 9- × 5-inch loaf pans.

6. After the dough has risen, gently punch it down in the bowl, releasing the air and moving the gasses around. Turn it out onto a lightly floured work surface. Using a long, sharp knife or bench scraper, cut it into two equal pieces. Shape each piece into a loaf and place in the prepared loaf pans. Cover the loaf pans with a tea towel and let rise in a warm, draft-free spot for up to 1 hour, or until the loaves have doubled in size.

7. Preheat the oven to 350°F 30 minutes before you're ready to bake.

8. Using a lame or very sharp knife, score the bread about ¼ inch deep a few times on a slight angle to give the accumulated air bubbles somewhere to go. Brush the loaves with the egg wash.

9. Bake, side by side, on the middle rack of the oven for 30 minutes. Rotate the pans 180 degrees to ensure they brown evenly. Bake for another 15 to 20 minutes, or until the internal temperature is 190°F and you hear a hollow sound when you tap the bottom of the pan.

10. Remove the bread from the loaf pan and let cool on a wire rack for 15 to 20 minutes before cutting. Toast until golden or serve as is.

NOTE: You can also bake this as three smaller loaves, if you like. Simply grease a large baking sheet, and shape the dough into three evenly sized loaves. Place them on the baking sheet a couple of inches apart, and bake for 20 minutes before rotating the pan 180 degrees. Bake for 10 more minutes before checking for doneness. The three smaller loaves will cook much faster than two larger loaves.

Lodge Kitchen Molasses Bread

I love the richness and deep, beautiful flavor that molasses brings to bread. In this recipe, it is also vital to the bread's moistness and denseness. This bread will take a sandwich from 0 to 60 in a split second. It works well alongside rich soups, and it looks beautiful at the dinner table.

MAKES 2 (9- × 5-INCH) LOAVES

Here's what you'll need:

Granulated sugar

1½ cups tap-hot water

1½ tablespoons active dry yeast

1 cup rolled oats

2 tablespoons salted butter, softened

2 teaspoons kosher salt

1½ cups boiling water

⅔ cup fancy molasses

6 cups all-purpose flour, plus extra for kneading

1 egg, beaten + 1 teaspoon water, for egg wash

Caraway seeds

Coarse salt

Here's how it's done:

1. In a small bowl or large measuring cup, dissolve a pinch of sugar in the warm water. Sprinkle in the yeast, stir very gently, and then let the mixture sit for about 8 to 10 minutes. When the yeast is bubbly and frothy, it is ready.

2. In a separate bowl, mix the oats with the butter and salt. Pour the boiling water overtop and mix well. Add the molasses, mix to incorporate, and let cool completely.

3. Add the yeast mixture and mix to combine. Add 6 cups of the flour, 1 cup at a time, mixing well between additions. If the dough is still very wet and sticky, gradually add more flour, 1 tablespoon at a time. Using a stiff spatula, mix everything until it feels a bit tacky but not too wet. It should be shaggy in both texture and appearance.

4. Turn the dough out onto a lightly floured work surface. Using both hands, knead the dough. Press the center of the dough with the heels of your hands, then push them onto the dough and away from you. Using quarter turns, pull the dough back toward you with the heels of your hands, adding only enough extra flour to keep the dough from sticking. Continue this process until you begin to feel air developing in the dough and it looks and feels smooth and slightly tacky and springs back when poked with your finger. This whole process should take between 8 and 10 minutes.

5. Lightly oil a large mixing bowl, place the dough in it, turning it over once to ensure the whole ball is covered in oil, and cover with a dry tea towel. Set aside in a warm, draft-free spot to rise for up to 1 hour, or until doubled in size.

6. After the bread has risen, gently punch it down in the bowl, releasing the air and moving the gasses around. Remove from the bowl, turn onto a lightly floured work surface, and knead for 6 to 8 minutes, just as you did before.

7. Grease two 9- × 5-inch loaf pans.

8. Using a long, sharp knife or bench scraper, cut the dough in half and shape each piece to fit your loaf pans, pinching the seam closed. Place the loaves, seam side down, in the loaf pans. Cover the loaf pans with a dry tea towel and let rise in a warm, draft-free spot for up to 1 hour, or until the loaves have doubled in size.

9. Preheat the oven to 350°F halfway through this rising time.

10. Using a lame or razor, score the loaves ¼ inch deep and about 3 inches long a couple of times on a slight angle to give the accumulated air bubbles somewhere to go. Brush the surface of the bread with the egg wash and sprinkle lightly with a pinch of caraway seeds and salt.

11. Bake the loaves, side by side, on the middle rack of the oven for 45 to 55 minutes, turning once halfway, or until the internal temperature has reached 190°F and the bread makes a hollow sound when you tap the bottom of the pan. Remove from the loaf pans and place on a wire rack to cool.

12. This bread is too delicious to last long, so make sure you grab yourself a hot buttered slice once you've allowed it to cool slightly on a wire rack.

Skiers' Hearty Seed Bread

I make a lot of bread—a couple of tons every season, most likely. In my experience, one of the best trail breads of all time is this seed bread. People love sturdy sandwich bread they can take out with them for a few—or more—hours without worrying that it will get soggy and or lose its allure. In this recipe, the bread gets its gorgeous crust and crumb from being baked in a Dutch oven.

MAKES 1 LARGE LOAF

Here's what you'll need:

Granulated sugar

1½ cups warm water

1 tablespoon active dry yeast

2 tablespoons brown flax seeds

1½ tablespoons golden sesame seeds,
  plus extra for garnish

1½ teaspoons poppy seeds, plus extra for garnish

1 teaspoon vegetable oil, plus extra for coating

Coarse salt

2 tablespoons pumpkin seeds

2 tablespoons sunflower seeds

3 cups all-purpose flour, plus extra for kneading

2 tablespoons liquid honey

2 teaspoons kosher salt, plus extra for sprinkling

Cornmeal, for dusting

1 egg, beaten + 1 teaspoon water, for egg wash

Here's how it's done:

1. In a small bowl, dissolve a pinch of sugar in the warm water. Sprinkle the yeast in, stir very gently, and then let the mixture sit for about 8 to 10 minutes. When the yeast is bubbly and frothy, it is ready.

2. In a cast iron pan over medium heat, toast the flax, sesame and poppy seeds until golden and the flax seeds are beginning to crackle and give off a nutty fragrance, about 3 minutes. Transfer to a bowl and allow to cool.

3. Add the oil and a pinch of coarse salt to the pan and toast the pumpkin and sunflower seeds until they give off a sweet, nutty aroma, about 5 to 6 minutes. Add them to the bowl with the other seeds to cool.

4. In a mixing bowl, mix the flour with the honey and kosher salt. Add the toasted seeds and mix everything together. Make a well in the middle of the dry mixture and pour the yeast mixture into it. Fold the dry ingredients into the wet until you have a lumpy, shaggy dough with no dry spots of flour, about 2 minutes.

5. Turn the dough out onto a lightly floured work surface. Using both hands, knead the dough. Press the center of the dough with the heels of your hands, then push them onto the dough and away from you. Using quarter turns, pull the dough back toward you with the heels of your hands, adding only enough extra flour to keep the dough from sticking. Continue this process until you begin to feel air developing in the dough and it is smooth and springs back when poked with your finger. If not, knead for a couple more minutes. This whole process should take between 8 and 10 minutes.

6. Scrape down the bread bowl and discard any stuck pieces. Lightly oil a large mixing bowl, place the dough in it, turning once to ensure the whole ball is covered in oil, and cover with a dry tea towel. Set aside in a warm, draft-free spot to rise for up to 1 hour, or until doubled in size.

7. After the dough has risen, gently punch it down in the bowl, releasing the air and moving the gasses around. Turn it out onto a lightly floured work surface and knead again for 8 to 10 minutes, until it becomes a smooth ball. Gently push the dough away from you and then roll it up into a cylinder, tucking your fingers into the dough as you roll. Turn the dough over and seal the seam by pinching it along the length. Pinch the ends closed as well.

8. Place a piece of parchment paper on your work surface and give it a light coating of oil. Dust with cornmeal, shaking off any excess. Place the shaped dough on top of the parchment, cover with a tea towel, and let rise again for 1 hour, or until doubled in size.

9. Place a Dutch oven with a 12-inch diameter, about 3 to 4 inches deep, with the lid on, in the oven and preheat to 450°F.

10. Using a lame or razor, score the bread about ¼ inch deep and 3 inches long a couple of times on a slight angle or in a decorative pattern to give the accumulated air bubbles somewhere to go. Brush the entire surface of the loaf with the egg wash and sprinkle with some sesame and poppy seeds, and coarse salt.

11. To prepare for the transfer of the dough to the Dutch oven, place a trivet on the counter or heat-safe ceramic tile. Cut a piece of parchment into a rectangular shape, longer than it is wide, essentially making "handles" so you can safely lower the dough into the Dutch oven. Place the parchment on top of a clean baking sheet and transfer the dough, quickly but gently, to sit on top of the parchment.

12. Once the oven has reached temperature, carefully remove the Dutch oven and place on the trivet. Take off the lid and place it on a heat-resistant surface. Wearing heat-resistant gloves or oven mitts, lift the sides of the parchment and place the dough in the bottom of the hot Dutch oven, still on the parchment. You might need to wiggle the dough into place. Cover the Dutch oven and bake the bread on the center rack of the oven for 30 minutes.

13. Wearing oven mitts, carefully reach into the oven and remove the lid without bringing the Dutch oven out of the heat (tricky but not impossible). Bake, uncovered, for another 15 to 20 minutes, or until the top of the bread is gloriously golden and the internal temperature is 190°F. Transfer the bread to a wire rack to cool completely before slicing.

Quinoa Bread

This bread recipe uses a sponge or yeast starter made with commercially prepared yeast, rather than a sourdough starter, which is made with wild yeast. The sponge for this recipe is made ahead of time, allowing it to ferment before the rest of the ingredients are added in, so you can't make this bread on a whim—you have to prep this the night before you plan to eat it. The whole process is worth the wait, though, as this bread has a wonderful depth of flavor and a light texture.

MAKES 3 (9- × 5-INCH) LOAVES

Here's what you'll need:

SPONGE:

3 cups tap-hot water

1 tablespoon liquid honey

1 tablespoon molasses

2½ teaspoons instant yeast

2 cups all-purpose flour

2 cups whole wheat flour

¼ cup vegetable oil

BREAD:

3 cups whole wheat flour

1 cup all-purpose flour, plus extra for kneading

2 cups cooked red and white quinoa

Kosher salt

1 egg + 1 teaspoon water, for egg wash

1 tablespoon uncooked quinoa

Here's how it's done:

1. To make the sponge, place the water in a medium mixing bowl. Add the honey and molasses and, using a wooden spoon, stir to dissolve. Add the yeast, stir gently to incorporate, and then mix in both flours, 1 cup at a time, for 3 to 4 minutes, switching to a spatula to scrape down the sides of the bowl as required. The batter will be sticky and elastic.

2. Cover the bowl with plastic wrap and refrigerate overnight.

3. Take the sponge out of the fridge, give it a quick stir with a wooden spoon, and cover with a tea towel instead of the plastic wrap. Leave it to sit at room temperature until it doubles in size, about 1 hour. Don't allow it to get too big or it will collapse on itself.

4. Make a small well in the middle of the sponge and add the oil. Using a sturdy spatula or wooden spoon, fold and blend until the oil is completely absorbed.

5. To make the bread, in a large mixing bowl, mix together both flours, cooked quinoa, and a large pinch of salt. Add the sponge and stir well until blended. Using your hands, knead the dough in the bowl until all the ingredients are fully combined.

6. Turn the dough out onto a lightly floured work surface. Using both hands, knead the dough. Press the center of the dough with the heels of your hands, then push them onto the dough and away from you. Using quarter turns, pull the dough back toward you with the heels of your hands, adding only enough extra flour to keep the dough from sticking. Continue this process until you begin to feel air developing in the dough and it is smooth and slightly tacky and springs back when poked with your finger. This whole process should take between 8 and 10 minutes.

7. Lightly oil a large mixing bowl, place the dough in it, turning once to ensure the whole ball is covered in oil, and cover with a tea towel. Set aside in a warm, draft-free spot to rise for up to 1 hour, or until doubled in size.

8. Grease three 9- × 5-inch loaf pans.

9. After the dough has risen, gently punch it down in the bowl, releasing the air and moving the gasses around. Turn it out onto a lightly floured work surface. Using a long, sharp knife or bench scraper, cut it into two equal pieces. Shape each piece into a loaf and place in the prepared loaf pans. Cover the loaf pans with a tea towel and set aside in a warm, draft-free spot to rise for up to 1 hour, or until the loaves have doubled in size.

10. Preheat the oven to 375°F 30 minutes before you're ready to bake.

11. Using a lame or a very sharp knife, score the bread about ¼ inch deep and 2 inches long a few times on a slight angle to give the accumulated air bubbles somewhere to go. Brush the loaves with the egg wash and sprinkle the uncooked quinoa overtop.

12. Bake, side by side, on the middle rack of the oven for 45 to 60 minutes, rotating halfway through cooking. Bake until the internal temperature is 190°F. You can check if the bread is done by turning it over and tapping the bottom of the loaf. If it sounds hollow, then your bread is ready.

13. Remove the bread from the loaf pan and cool on a wire rack before serving it with butter!

NOTE: If you must have the bread the day you make the sponge, you can set the sponge aside on the countertop, covered with plastic wrap, for 2 hours or up to 8 hours.

The Simplest of Sourdough Starters

When I first started making my own bread, a friend told me all about starters—sourdough starters, leavens, mothers, barms, and so on. I was fascinated. I could not wait to catch and tame my own wild yeast. I thought of how I could travel with my starter, share it with friends, build a local starter club—the possibilities seemed endless. But then life got in the way.

Over the past couple of seasons, though, I have gotten back into the swing of things, mainly because the enthusiastic lodge staff I work with have fallen in love with the flavors of the breads that begin with a wild yeast starter, just as I once did. I didn't realize how much I missed the process until I was once again working and loving and nurturing a friendly little sourdough starter.

A starter is simply a combination of flour and water that has been colonized by wild yeast, which lives in the air around us. The starter is then fermented and ultimately it becomes a leavening agent, or leaven. The leaven is added to the bread dough to promote further fermentation and make the bread rise, and it's added in place of commercially prepared yeast—the type you find at a grocery store and that is a by-product of whiskey distillers.

To be well developed, a starter needs time and patience and a regular feeding schedule to create the right consistency, moisture, aeration, acidity, flavors, and so on. Allow it to develop for 5 to 7 days before you plan on using it. This is worth it, though, as it creates a more interesting crust and crumb texture and adds more depth of flavor than regular processed or yeasted breads. And once you have an established starter, you can maintain it and nurture it for generations to come. You can use this starter recipe in Backcountry Sourdough Bread (page 109).

MAKES 1 SOURDOUGH STARTER

Here's what you'll need for each feeding:

¾ cup all-purpose flour
½ cup chlorine-free water, at room temperature

Here's how it's done:

You need a nonreactive bowl or a glass jar with at least a 8-cup capacity and that you can cover easily without making it airtight (for example, by draping a dry towel over it and fixing it in place with an elastic band), so that the starter gets the oxygen it needs. I use a large glass jar so that I can see the starter bubbling and rising up the sides. Also, if your water is chlorinated, you can leave the water out the night before so the chlorine evaporates or you can use water that has been boiled and then cooled—basically don't use chlorinated water, otherwise you'll kill the microorganisms and good bacteria that are needed for the wild yeast to thrive.

DAY 1: Place the flour in a large, nonreactive bowl or glass jar and, using a small whisk or fork, gradually mix in the water until there is no dry flour showing and the batter is smooth and tacky. You may need to add an extra tablespoon or so of flour or water to get the right texture.

Cover the bowl as indicated above and let sit, undisturbed, away from direct sunlight at room temperature for 24 hours. In the cooler months, I keep mine on top of the fridge (about 75°F). And that is it for Day 1.

DAY 2: Try to feed your starter at the same time every day. This establishes a relationship between the two of you and it also creates consistency. Using a sturdy spatula, scrape down the sides of the bowl. Add ¾ cup of flour (always use the same flour, from the same bag) and about ½ cup of room-temperature, chlorine-free water. The starter should be doughy and bubbly. If a sticky, thicker dough is desired, add 1 or 2 tablespoons more water. Using a small whisk or fork, mix vigorously until all the flour is incorporated. Cover and return to its resting spot.

DAY 3: Today might be a great day to name your starter! It would like that. Your starter should now be showing signs of activity—bubbles on top and on the sides, with a bit of a sour, pungent smell. If it isn't, don't fret. I've had some starters that I almost gave up on and then, on Day 4 or 5, they suddenly became amazingly active.

Follow the same steps as Day 2—but today you need to do them twice, about 12 hours apart. Yep! Two feedings a day. Same instructions and quantities for both feedings.

DAY 4: You will notice a big change in the starter today. The wild yeast in the flour will be eating the sugars in earnest and the starter should be releasing lots of tiny sponge-like bubbles. This is the carbon dioxide being released, and with this comes acidity, which creates the pungent, sour smell. This smell is a good thing. It means the starter is alive, thanks to your efforts. The acidity is also responsible for killing off any bad bacteria that may have been present right at the beginning. At this stage, you will also see the starter rising up the sides of the receptacle within a couple of hours of each feeding before taking time to go back down again. It is exciting to watch and makes you realize how quickly your starter has grown in such a short amount of time!

Before feeding your starter today, discard half of the contents. Then feed your starter with ¾ cup of all-purpose flour and ½ cup room-temperature, chlorine-free water. When you mix with a small whisk or fork, you will notice your starter has a lighter texture.

Follow the instructions from Day 3, feeding it twice, with 12 hours between feeds again, remembering to discard about half of the starter before feeding each time.

DAY 5: Today will most likely be the pinnacle of your success with the starter. You will notice a wonderfully nutty, sour smell and see not only an abundance of bubbles but also a dramatic and consistent rise for a couple of hours after each feeding. If you feel your starter is ready, you can use it today for baking. There are a couple of ways to determine the readiness of your starter. You can usually tell by assessing the activity in the starter itself. Just ask yourself, is it bubbly and quite spongy looking? Does it omit a somewhat strong, fresh, and sour smell? Is it lighter than previous days when you mix it, with a consistent lattice of bubbles throughout? If yes, it is almost certainly ready to bake with.

If you want to be 100% certain, you can also do the float test. Simply remove a scant tablespoon of sourdough starter and place it in a glass filled with room-temperature, chlorine-free water. If the starter floats, it is ready to go. If the starter sinks to the bottom, it will need a couple of more feedings. Just follow the feeding instructions from Day 4.

If your starter is not meeting your expectations, don't get discouraged. It could be that you need to move it to a warmer spot, or that it would benefit from a good and vigorous mixing. Sometimes aeration is the issue. Getting a lot of oxygen moving through the starter after each feeding will ensure it remains active. If you find an amber liquid has formed on top between feedings, simply mix it into the starter before you split off the unwanted starter and begin the day's feeding process. The liquid, referred to as "hooch," is a by-product of the fermentation process. It is very common but it needs to be incorporated back into the starter to keep the starter viscous. It will also help build the starter's appetite, making your feedings more important.

Once you start using the starter as a leavening agent, you can move it to the fridge. Just make sure to feed and nourish your starter after each use by discarding all but half, feeding as per usual, and allowing it to rise for about 3 hours at room temperature before placing it in an airtight container with enough room for your starter to continue to rise in the fridge. This is essential if you plan on baking only once a week or every couple of weeks, in order to keep it healthy and vital.

Established starters will live for days on end without being fed, so you don't need to continue with daily feeding, but if you love yours and want it to be your trusted friend, don't leave it for too long in the fridge. If you are going away, it will be fine in the fridge for a couple of weeks. Just make sure to show it some love upon your return.

When you plan on using your starter again after a longer period of time, it is important to remove it from the fridge about 48 hours before you plan on using it. Mix it well with a whisk or fork, discard half, and feed it ¾ cup all-purpose flour and about ½ cup room-temperature, chlorine-free water. Let rest, covered with a towel held in place by an elastic band. You will be amazed to see how your starter will wake up and become active once again. Continue this method until you have the tell-tale signs that it is ready to act as a leaven in your recipe.

Backcountry Sourdough Bread

So, you've got your sourdough starter (page 106) and now you need a sourdough bread recipe that is both dependable and spectacular. This is the recipe for you. It might seem a bit complicated, but I know that after you have tried it a handful of times, you will not need to race to the recipe every single time. The steps and movements will become ingrained in your memory, and you will only look at this recipe now and again to remind you of how far you have come down the sourdough path of life! (Note that you need to begin this two nights before you plan to bake it.)

MAKES 2 LOAVES

Here's what you'll need:

LEAVEN:

1 tablespoon active sourdough starter (page 106)

½ cup all-purpose flour

⅓ cup tap-hot, chlorine-free water

DOUGH:

1 tablespoon kosher salt

2½ cups tap-hot, chlorine-free water, divided

5 cups all-purpose flour, plus extra for kneading

Here's how it's done:

1. If your sourdough starter has been refrigerated, remove it from the fridge and stir to mix in any liquid sitting on top. Discard all but ½ cup of the starter. Feed it with ¾ cup of flour and about ¾ cup of warm, unchlorinated water (see page 106). Cover it loosely, let sit at room temperature for 12 hours, and feed again. It should have plenty of life again after these two feedings. (If it hasn't been refrigerated, you can skip this step as long as you have been keeping up with regular feedings.)

2. To make the leaven, place the flour and water in a medium bowl and add the 1 tablespoon of sourdough starter. Mix well to form a paste, cover tightly with plastic wrap, and let sit at room temperature overnight.

3. The next day, to make the dough, dissolve the salt in ½ cup of the water. Stir well so that the salt is completely dissolved. Set aside.

4. Pour the remaining 2 cups of water into the bowl with the leaven. Using a wooden spoon, spatula, or your hands, break down the leaven as much as possible. Don't whisk it, as this will affect the consistency.

5. Fold in 5 cups of the flour, 1 cup at a time, collecting all the flour after each addition so a shaggy dough ball begins to form. All the flour must be fully incorporated into the mix. Cover with a damp tea towel and let sit at room temperature for 30 minutes, or up to 4 hours. This stage, known as the autolyze stage, is crucial as it is when the flour absorbs all of the moisture from the bread dough, aiding in the formation of gluten. The breakdown of the enzymes and complex starches into sugars, adorably known as the "sugar factory workers," nourishes the yeast and the natural bacteria in the leaven, which improves the breads texture and flavor.

6. Add the salted water to the flour mixture. Using your hands, mix the water into the flour to incorporate. Begin to fold the sticky dough in the bowl. This will develop strength in the dough gently, unlike with the more traditional knead. The folding will also release the carbon dioxides created in the fermentation process, which will elongate the gluten strands and make your dough stronger. Lift up the dough, fold it over onto itself, and move the bowl 360 degrees twice, working in quarter turns, and giving the dough a light dusting of flour if it is too wet. Remember, you are not preparing the dough like a yeasted bread. You simply need to fold it to combine the contents of the bowl. From here on, fold the dough every 30 minutes for the next 2 hours, for a total of five folds including the first. You will notice by the third and fourth fold that the dough has acquired a more taut texture that is smooth and elastic. It will spring back when poked with your finger.

7. Once you've finished the folding, leave the dough to rest in the bowl, uncovered, at room temperature for 1 hour. The dough will not necessarily rise to double its size like a commercially yeasted bread, but it will still proof and develop more structure and volume.

recipe continues

8. To prepare the bowls for the final stage, coat two bowls lined with clean tea towels (or two proofing baskets) with a heaping amount of all-purpose flour to prevent your loaves from sticking to the towel. Some people swear by rye flour; others prefer a rice flour and all-purpose flour combination. The more proficient you become with sourdough, the more you will feel like playing around with different techniques and ingredients. For now, all-purpose flour will be fine.

9. Turn the dough out onto a lightly floured work surface. Using a long, sharp knife or bench scraper, cut it into two evenly sized pieces. Lift and fold the dough again a couple of times to achieve some tension. Take one of the loaves and lift the lip, pulling it up as you do, and fold it over toward the center. Repeat this step, turning the loaf in quarter turns, until you have gone around the loaf once. Turn the loaf over. Brush away any flour left on your work surface. Lightly flour your hands, and this time tuck the dough underneath itself. Continue folding the dough underneath itself, tucking it under five or six times to create a nice smooth surface on the top.

10. Cup the loaf on either side, placing your thumbs on top. Starting with the side where your pinky finger is, shimmy the dough back and forth in a rocking motion to achieve more surface tension. Continue to cup it and rock it, gently tucking the sides underneath itself, turning it in a circular pattern as you tighten it up further. This entire step should only take about 30 to 40 seconds.

11. Using a bench scraper, or your lightly floured hands, turn the dough over in one fell swoop and place it in your prepared bowl or proofing basket. Repeat steps 9 to 11 with the second loaf.

12. Coat both loaves with all-purpose flour, covering the tops and the sides where possible. This will prevent the plastic from sticking during the final proof. Cover with plastic wrap and let rise for 3 hours at room temperature. Alternatively, you can rest the shaped loaves overnight in the fridge, wrapped tightly in a clean plastic bag, for up to 14 hours. If you are resting the loaves in the fridge, you can bake them without having to bring them back to room temperature. The dough will rise by not quite half, and will be airy and billowy.

13. Place two Dutch ovens with a 12-inch diameter, about 3 to 4 inches deep, in the oven with the lids on and preheat the oven to 500°F. Do not use baking pans that are not made of cast iron, as they can crack at high heat. (If you don't have two Dutch ovens, make this bread in batches, or use a Pyrex dish with a fitted lid.) If you bake the bread in batches, just leave the uncooked loaf tightly covered until you are prepared to use it.

14. To prepare for the transfer of the dough to the Dutch oven, place a large trivet on the counter or heat-safe ceramic tile. Cut a piece of parchment into a rectangular shape, longer than it is wide, essentially making "handles" so you can safely lower the dough into the Dutch oven. Place the parchment on top of a clean baking sheet and transfer the dough, quickly but gently, to sit on top of the parchment.

15. Using a fine sieve, lightly dust the tops of the loaves with all-purpose flour or rice flour. Using a lame or razor, score the bread about ¼ inch deep and about 3 inches long a couple of times on a slight angle or in a decorative pattern to give the accumulated air bubbles somewhere to go.

16. Once the oven has reached temperature, carefully remove the Dutch ovens and place on the trivet. Take off the lid off one pot and place it on a heat-resistant surface. Wearing heat-resistant gloves or oven mitts, lift the sides of the parchment and place the dough in the bottom of the hot Dutch oven while it is still on the parchment. You might need to wiggle the dough into place. Repeat with the second loaf.

17. Cover the Dutch ovens and bake the loaves, side by side, on the center rack for 20 minutes. Turn down the heat to 450°F and bake for another 10 minutes. Wearing oven mitts, carefully reach into the oven and remove the lids without bringing the Dutch ovens out of the heat (tricky but not impossible). Bake, uncovered, for another 15 to 20 minutes, or until the tops are a deep golden brown, the slashes form crisp ridges, and the internal temperature is 200°F.

18. Remove the Dutch ovens and let sit for about 10 minutes. Carefully transfer the bread to a wire rack, and cool for at least 30 minutes.

19. This does get easier with time, I promise. It becomes almost ritualistic, and you will find that the steps seem increasingly less complicated. Now, enjoy your success and celebrate the gorgeous loaves you prepared!

Val's Twisty Cheesy Buns

Val became a backcountry lodge chef in the early 80s. She is one of the most creative and interesting chefs in the industry and has introduced both staff and guests to many incredible and delicious recipes. This recipe for her cheesy twirls is an all-time favorite of mine. It might seem a bit intimidating at first, what with all the folding and twisting, but the results are so worth the effort.

MAKES 8–10 BUNS

Here's what you'll need:

1 cup 2% milk

4 tablespoons granulated sugar, divided

2 tablespoons active dry yeast

3 cups all-purpose flour, plus extra for kneading

1 teaspoon kosher salt

8 tablespoons salted butter, cold, cubed

3 egg yolks

3 tablespoons salted butter, melted

1½ cups grated sharp white cheddar cheese

2 tablespoons fresh thyme leaves

Ground black pepper

1 egg, beaten + 1 teaspoon water, for egg wash

Here's how it's done:

1. In a saucepan over medium heat, gently warm the milk, but do not bring to even a simmer. Remove from the heat and add 2 tablespoons of the sugar. Stir to dissolve the sugar, sprinkle the yeast in, stir very gently, and then let the mixture sit for about 8 to 10 minutes. When the yeast is bubbly and frothy, it is ready.

2. In a food processor, pulse the remaining 2 tablespoons of sugar, flour, and salt to just combine. Add the butter and pulse to make a coarse mixture. (If you do not have a food processor, use a pastry cutter or two forks.)

3. With the machine running, add the egg yolks. Process until the mixture is smooth and sticky. Transfer it to a large mixing bowl and add the yeast mixture. Using your hands, bring the dough together until you have a lumpy, shaggy dough with no dry spots of flour, about 2 minutes.

4. Turn the dough out onto a lightly floured work surface, adding extra flour as necessary to keep the dough from sticking. Using both hands, knead the dough. Press the center of the dough with the heels of your hands, then push them onto the dough and away from you. Using quarter turns, pull the dough back toward you with the heels of your hands, adding only enough extra flour to keep the dough from sticking. Continue this process until you begin to feel air developing in the dough and it is smooth and slightly tacky and springs back when poked with your finger. This whole process should take between 8 and 10 minutes.

5. Lightly oil a large mixing bowl, place the dough in it, turning once to ensure the whole ball is covered in oil, and cover with plastic wrap. Refrigerate for at least 4 hours, or up to overnight.

recipe continues

6. Preheat the oven to 375°F. Line two baking sheets with parchment paper.

7. Remove the dough from the fridge and allow it to sit for 10 minutes. Using a rolling pin, roll it out into an 18- × 15-inch rectangle. Lightly dust the dough with flour if the rolling pin is sticking. Work slowly if you are encountering air bubbles.

8. Brush the dough with the melted butter and sprinkle the cheese overtop. Sprinkle with the thyme and pepper to taste.

9. Fold the dough in half horizontally. Using your fingers, pinch together the long edges where they meet, ensuring everything is held fast.

10. Roll the dough out again, this time to about an 18- × 10-inch rectangle. You may find some more air bubbles under the surface—work these out slowly so the dough doesn't rupture.

11. Using a long, sharp knife or bench scraper, cut the dough into 10-inch-long, ½-inch-wide strips. You should get 16 to 20 strips. Pinch the tops of 2 strips to keep them together. Twist the two pieces around each other until they are closely but not tightly wound. Holding the end down, wrap the twisted dough around itself so it is circular and flat. Pinch the loose end tightly to the underside of the bun and place on a prepared baking sheet.

12. Brush the buns with the egg wash and bake, side by side, on the middle rack of the oven for 20 to 25 minutes, rotating them 180 degrees halfway through to ensure they brown evenly.

13. Remove from the baking sheets and let cool on a wire rack. I sometimes put a piece of butter on them as they come out of the oven to melt overtop.

Focaccia with Love

Focaccia is a flat, Italian-style bread that is seasoned with olive oil and topped with all kinds of really yummy stuff. This recipe uses a mix of classic and contemporary focaccia ingredients. It is easy to pull together, although it is best to get started on it the evening prior to serving it so you look like a total focaccia pro in front of all your climbing buddies. Use the best extra virgin olive oil you can get your hands on for this one.

MAKES 1 (13- × 9-INCH) FOCACCIA

Here's what you'll need:

DOUGH:

3½ cups all-purpose flour, plus extra for kneading

Kosher salt

2 teaspoons granulated sugar

1½ cups tap-hot water

2 teaspoons active dry yeast

½ cup extra virgin olive oil, plus extra for the bowl

2 garlic cloves, minced

1 tablespoon fresh rosemary leaves

1 tablespoon fresh thyme leaves

Ground black pepper

Cornmeal, for dusting

TOPPING:

1 tablespoon extra virgin olive oil

Maldon salt

1 cup roughly chopped artichoke hearts

½ cup red onion, thinly sliced

½ cup pitted and sliced green olives

¼ cup pitted and sliced Kalamata olives

1 rosemary sprig, leaves only

Ground black pepper

Here's how it's done:

1. To make the dough, in a mixing bowl, mix 3½ cups of the flour with a pinch of salt. Make a well in the center and sprinkle in the sugar, followed by the water. Stir to dissolve the sugar. Sprinkle in the yeast, stir very gently, and then let the mixture sit for about 8 to 10 minutes. When the yeast is bubbly and foamy, it is ready. Stir with a wooden spoon until all the ingredients have formed a shaggy dough, with no dry bits of flour.

2. Meanwhile, in a saucepan over medium heat, warm the oil. Add the garlic, rosemary, thyme, and pepper to taste. Sauté for about 5 to 6 minutes, or until the garlic starts to soften and brown slightly. Remove from the heat and let cool for a couple of minutes.

3. Slowly fold the cooled oil and herbs into the dough. Using your hands, pinch and squeeze the dough to work in the oil and herbs and combine all the ingredients. Add a pinch or two more of flour if the dough is too sticky.

4. Turn the dough out onto a work surface (do not flour the surface at this point or the dough will become too dry). Knead the dough, using both hands. Press the center of the dough with the heels of your hands, then push them onto the dough and away from you. Using quarter turns, pull the dough back toward you with the heels of your hands. Continue this process until you begin to feel air developing in the dough and it is smooth and tacky and springs back when poked with your finger. This whole process should take between 8 and 10 minutes.

recipe continues

5. Lightly oil a large mixing bowl, place the dough in it, turning once to ensure the whole ball is covered in oil, and cover with plastic wrap. Set aside in a warm, draft-free spot to rise for up to 1 hour, or refrigerate overnight. If you refrigerate the dough overnight, be sure to take it out of the fridge at least 40 minutes before beginning the next stage.

6. Turn the dough out onto a lightly floured work surface and gently roll it out to a 13- × 9-inch rectangle, working the air bubbles out as you go. Cover with a clean tea towel. Let rise on the work surface for about 40 minutes, or until doubled in size.

7. Preheat the oven to 425°F. Lightly oil a 13- × 9-inch baking sheet and sprinkle generously with cornmeal, shaking off any excess like Taylor Swift.

8. Lift the dough onto the baking sheet, and push it and work it so it fits the sheet like a glove. Using your fingertips, work your way around and over the entire surface, making dimple marks. Don't go all the way through the dough, just poke and prod it a bit.

9. Brush the dough with the 1 tablespoon of oil and sprinkle lavishly with some Maldon salt.

10. Arrange the artichokes, onion, olives, and rosemary on the dough. Finish with pepper to taste.

11. Bake on the middle rack of the oven for 20 to 25 minutes, or until the focaccia has begun to turn golden brown and the toppings are delightfully roasted.

12. Let cool on the pan for 1 to 2 minutes and then use a large spatula to transfer it to a wire rack to cool for a wee bit longer. Lift onto a large cutting board and cut to the desired size.

NOTE: Sliced pimento-stuffed olives also make for a lovely topping.

Mistaya Lodge

Talk about exhilarating. This place has it all: pristine peaks, ten gorgeous glaciers, and a lifetime of alpine meadows. Indoors, the lodge boasts an open kitchen, where the lodge chef offers delicious meals and wine and, if you are so inclined, allows you to assist and demonstrate your own kitchen prowess . . . but first you have to ski or hike to earn your place at the table!

Located in the Wild Cat Basin at 6,700 feet, Mistaya Lodge delivers on priceless views of the surrounding peaks and glaciers from the cozy living room or from out on the expansive deck.

The lodge was built in the 1980s, and has since undergone several renovations to improve on its environmental footprint and to make the lodge guests more comfortable and pampered. The hosts, Cindy and Dave, have installed a micro-hydro system, built a small and well-producing greenhouse, and made every effort to do all of their lodge shopping locally. Their passion never wavers, which you can see for yourself in all of the details and the cozy rooms.

The indoors speaks of comfort and relaxation, and the outdoors is recognized for its fantastic skiing and untracked terrain. You will see no one up there besides your local lodge mates, so the place feels incredibly secluded and immense. A stay there can include heavenly skiing on cloud-like powder, snow angels, hiking boundless meadows and alpine lakes, wilderness photography, watercolor painting, or all of the above.

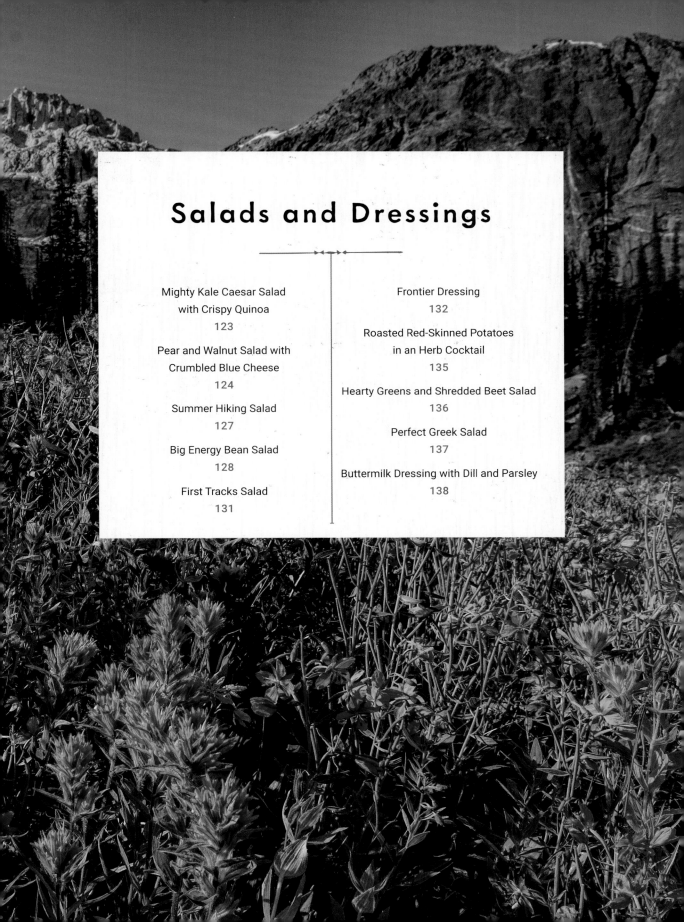

Salads and Dressings

Mighty Kale Caesar Salad with Crispy Quinoa

Caesar salad has an absolutely timeless quality to it. In this recipe, the kale adds extra texture and heartiness, and the oven-roasted quinoa brings something playful and unexpected to this mighty classic.

SERVES 4

Here's what you'll need:

½ cup uncooked quinoa (a mix of colors is fun)

1 cup chicken stock

1 large romaine lettuce

5–6 kale leaves, stems removed

2 garlic cloves

2–4 anchovies (optional)

¼ cup extra virgin olive oil

¼ cup vegetable oil

¼ cup apple cider vinegar

1 teaspoon smooth Dijon mustard

1 teaspoon Worcestershire sauce

Hot sauce

Kosher salt and cracked black pepper

¾ cup grated Parmigiano-Reggiano cheese, divided, plus extra for garnish (garnish optional)

2 eggs, at room temperature

½ lemon

Here's how it's done:

1. Rinse the quinoa in a sieve and shake off any excess water. Place it in a medium saucepan with a tight-fitting lid over medium-high heat. Add the stock and bring to a rolling boil. Turn down the heat immediately to low, cover, and cook for 12 minutes (the quinoa will finish cooking in the oven). Drain the quinoa and put it back in the pot to rest, uncovered, for 10 minutes.

2. Preheat the oven to 250°F. Lightly grease a baking sheet.

3. Stir the quinoa to break it up a bit, pour out onto the prepared baking sheet, and set aside to cool, moving the grains around occasionally.

4. Wash the lettuce and kale, dry them, and tear into large, evenly sized pieces. Place them in a bowl, cover loosely, and refrigerate.

5. Toast the quinoa, stirring and turning often, for about 1 hour, or until crispy. Remove from the oven, break up any clumps of quinoa, and set aside to cool.

6. In a blender, place the garlic, anchovies (if using), both oils, vinegar, Dijon, Worcestershire, a splash of hot sauce, and a pinch each of salt and pepper and blend to thoroughly combine. While the blender is running, slowly add ½ cup of the cheese. Blend until well combined again, but a few small bits are fine.

7. Cook the eggs in boiling water for about 1 minute. Remove from the water and let cool for 1 to 2 minutes, or until they are cool enough to peel. Add them to the blender, making sure to scrape all the whites in as well. Blend again and taste for seasoning.

8. To assemble the salad, toss the lettuce and kale with half of the dressing. Add the remaining ¼ cup of cheese and half of the quinoa. Toss again, adding more dressing if desired. Transfer to a serving bowl. Sprinkle with the remaining quinoa, more cheese (if desired), and the juice from the lemon half.

NOTE: The toasted quinoa stores really well in an airtight jar in the fridge for up to 1 week. It makes a terrific trail snack!

Pear and Walnut Salad with Crumbled Blue Cheese

In this recipe, the sweetness of the walnut and the tartness and texture of the pear complement the trademark blue cheese beautifully. This is a wonderful salad to enjoy on top of a mountain pass, looking down at the world.

SERVES 4

Here's what you'll need:

WALNUTS:

1 egg white

2½ cups walnut pieces

3 tablespoons granulated sugar

1¼ tablespoons brown sugar

Coarse salt

Ground cinnamon

Cayenne pepper

VINAIGRETTE:

1 garlic clove, crushed

¼ cup extra virgin olive oil

1½ tablespoons white wine vinegar

2 teaspoons liquid honey

1 teaspoon smooth Dijon mustard

Coarse salt and ground black pepper

½ teaspoon red pepper flakes

SALAD:

5–6 cups mixed greens, such as red and
  green lettuce, radicchio, frisée, endive

1 Bosc or Bartlett pear, unpeeled, cut in
  ¼-inch-thick slices

1¼ cups halved red grapes

⅔ cup crumbled blue cheese

Here's how it's done:

1. Preheat the oven to 300°F. Line a baking sheet with parchment paper.

2. To make the walnuts, in a mixing bowl, beat the egg white until frothy. Add 2 teaspoons of water and whisk to combine.

3. Place the walnut pieces in a medium mixing bowl.

4. In a separate small bowl, toss together both sugars, and a pinch each of salt, cinnamon, and cayenne. Add the spices to the egg white, mix to incorporate, and then pour over the walnuts pieces. Toss to coat the walnuts evenly and transfer to the prepared baking sheet, spreading them out in an even layer.

5. Bake for 15 to 20 minutes, tossing and moving occasionally so that they brown evenly and don't stick. When they start to caramelize and crisp up, they are done. Set aside to cool.

6. To make the vinaigrette, place the garlic, oil, vinegar, honey, Dijon, and salt and pepper to taste in a jar. Put the lid on the jar and shake to blend well. Add the red pepper flakes and shake again.

7. To make the salad, place the mixed greens, pear slices, and grapes in a serving bowl. Add the dressing and toss gently. Add the crumbled blue cheese, toss gently to distribute it evenly among the leaves, and top with the toasted, candied walnuts.

Summer Hiking Salad

The combination of colors from the quinoa, chèvre, spinach, mandarin, and red onion makes this a visually stunning salad, and the crunch of the almonds takes it up a notch on the texture ladder.

SERVES 4

Here's what you'll need:

SALAD:

⅓ cup slivered almonds

2 Roma tomatoes, cut into wedges

1 medium English cucumber, cubed

1 small red onion, halved and thinly sliced

6 cups baby spinach

1–1½ cups chèvre

1 (8.25 oz) can mandarins, drained

6–8 basil leaves, chiffonade

QUINOA:

½ cup red quinoa

1 cup chicken stock

DRESSING:

2 tablespoons grapeseed oil

2 tablespoons balsamic vinegar

½-inch piece ginger, peeled

2 garlic cloves, minced

Kosher salt and ground black pepper

Here's how it's done:

1. Preheat the oven to 350°F.

2. Place the almonds on a baking sheet and toast for 10 to 12 minutes, shaking the pan to mix things up halfway through. Remove from the oven and let cool.

3. To make the quinoa, rinse it in a sieve and shake off any excess water. Place it in a medium saucepan with a tight-fitting lid over medium-high heat. Add the stock and bring to a rolling boil on. Turn down the heat immediately to low, cover, and cook for 15 minutes. Once cooked, fluff the quinoa with a fork and let cool in the pot for 10 to 15 minutes.

4. To make the dressing, in a salad bowl, whisk together 2 tablespoons of the oil with the balsamic. Grate the ginger right into the vinegar and oil, and then add the garlic, and a pinch each of salt and pepper.

5. To prepare the salad, add the tomatoes, cucumber, and onion to the salad bowl. Toss well to coat with the dressing.

6. Add the quinoa, spinach, chèvre, mandarins, and basil. Toss the salad lightly and sprinkle the toasted almonds overtop before serving.

Big Energy Bean Salad

We all have those days outdoors when we could use a little pick-me-up to get to the top of a peak and back down. This salad makes a terrific packed lunch and offers an abundance of protein, vitamins, and fiber to give your body the energy and nutrition it needs to get you through any activity.

SERVES 6

Here's what you'll need:

SALAD:

1 (15.5 oz) can chickpeas, drained and rinsed

1 (15.5 oz) can kidney beans, drained and rinsed

1 (15.5 oz) can black beans, drained and rinsed

2 cups fresh green beans

3 celery stalks, cleaned and chopped

1 small red onion, diced

1 yellow bell pepper, chopped

1 red bell pepper, chopped

¼ cup chopped broccolini

4 green onions, chopped

Black sesame seeds

DRESSING:

¼ cup apple cider vinegar

¼ cup rice wine vinegar

⅓ cup granulated sugar

½ cup grapeseed oil

2 garlic cloves, minced

½ teaspoon ground cumin

Coarse salt and ground black pepper

Here's how it's done:

1. To make the salad, place the chickpeas, canned and fresh beans, celery, onion, bell pepper, and broccolini in a large mixing bowl. Set aside.

2. To make the dressing, in a saucepan over low heat, gently warm both vinegars. Add the sugar and bring to a boil to dissolve the sugar. Remove from the heat and let cool, whisking before serving.

3. In a mixing bowl, whisk the oil with the garlic, cumin, and salt and pepper to taste. Whisk in the cooled vinegar mixture. Pour the dressing over the beans and vegetables. Scatter the green onions overtop for some dazzle and garnish with a sprinkle of black sesame seeds.

First Tracks Salad

This salad feels like a dish for a celebration, with its many textures and colors. It looks almost as festive as the first day back on skis after a huge snowfall feels. Life really doesn't get much better than when you get to enjoy both on the same day.

SERVES 4

Here's what you'll need:

SALAD:

2 tablespoons black sesame seeds

2 tablespoons white sesame seeds

4 carrots, grated

2 ripe avocados, diced

1 lemon, juiced

2 cups arugula

½ red cabbage, shredded

½ cup chopped cilantro

3 green onions, chopped

DRESSING:

½ cup extra virgin olive oil

¼ cup apple cider vinegar

2 tablespoons honey

1-inch piece ginger, peeled and grated

Kosher salt and ground black pepper

Here's how it's done:

1. To prepare the salad, in a small skillet over medium heat, toast both sets of sesame seeds for about 5 to 6 minutes, or until the white sesame seeds have some color. Set aside in a bowl to cool.

2. Place the carrots and avocado in a salad bowl and drizzle with the lemon juice to keep them from browning. Add the arugula, cabbage, and cilantro and toss gently.

3. I like to make this dressing right before I serve the salad because of the flavor of the freshly grated ginger. In a jar, place the oil, vinegar, and honey. Give it a good shake. Add the ginger, and a pinch each of salt and pepper, and shake well again.

4. Dress the salad with the vinaigrette and sprinkle the sesame seeds and green onions overtop.

Frontier Dressing

I always have a flavorful dressing in the fridge to use for a quick salad topping or marinade, or to drizzle over roasted vegetables. This dressing is terrific for making late suppers after a big day out a little bit special.

MAKES ABOUT 1¼ CUPS

Here's what you'll need:

⅓ cup extra virgin olive oil

⅓ cup canola oil

¼ cup white wine vinegar

2 tablespoons liquid honey or agave nectar

1 tablespoon lemon juice

2 cloves garlic, minced

3 tablespoons grated Parmigiano-Reggiano cheese

1 teaspoon coarse salt

½ teaspoon red pepper flakes

½ teaspoon dried oregano

½ teaspoon dried parsley

½ teaspoon dried thyme leaves

½ teaspoon dried basil

Ground black pepper

Here's how it's done:

1. In a jar, place both oils, the vinegar, honey, and lemon juice. Shake well. Add the garlic and cheese and shake well again. Add the salt, red pepper flakes, oregano, parsley, thyme, basil, and pepper to taste. Shake until completely combined. Adjust the seasonings to taste, if necessary.

2. This dressing will keep in an airtight container in the fridge for a couple of weeks.

NOTE: If you prefer to use fresh herbs, you can double or triple the amounts but the dressing will need to be used within 1 week.

Roasted Red-Skinned Potatoes in an Herb Cocktail

Potato salad is one of those wonderful summer sides we long for as soon as we start to fire up the grill at the beginning of summer. With this recipe, you will be thinking potato salad year-round. It's also a terrific lunch idea for your next hike.

SERVES 4

Here's what you'll need:

2 lb baby red-skinned potatoes

2½ tablespoons extra virgin olive oil, divided

1 teaspoon dried rosemary

1 teaspoon kosher salt

1 tablespoon salted butter

¾ cup full-fat mayonnaise

2 teaspoons smooth Dijon mustard

2 teaspoons lemon juice

½ cup chopped green onion

½ cup chopped fresh dill leaves

½ cup chopped fresh flat-leaf or curly parsley

½ teaspoon red pepper flakes

½ cup chopped gherkins, for garnish

¼ cup chopped fresh mint leaves, for garnish

Here's how it's done:

1. Preheat the oven to 400°F.

2. Halve any larger potatoes lengthwise. Leave the others whole. Toss them in a bowl with 1½ tablespoons of the oil, the rosemary, and kosher salt. Place them on a baking tray just large enough to hold them without crowding and roast for 20 minutes. Remove from the oven and scatter the butter around the potatoes.

3. Return the pan to the oven and roast the potatoes for about 10 more minutes, until fork-tender, giving them a single shake to distribute the seasonings and butter. Transfer to a serving dish to cool slightly.

4. In a food processor, place the remaining 1 tablespoon of oil, the mayonnaise, Dijon, and lemon juice. Blend to emulsify. Add the green onion, dill, parsley, and red pepper flakes. Process until everything is well blended but not overmixed; a few coarse pieces make for a wonderful texture. If you find the consistency is too thick, add 1 to 2 tablespoons of water and blend again.

5. Pour this dressing over the potatoes, and toss to evenly coat. Place in the fridge, uncovered, for 1 hour, or up to overnight, to let the flavors really meld together.

6. Garnish with the gherkins and mint.

Hearty Greens and Shredded Beet Salad

Shredded beet in a salad is always a lodge favorite. The earthy, almost sweet flavor, wonderful texture, and deep, natural color all bring an extravagant flair to the table. The vinaigrette in this salad is deliberately simple to allow the beets to steal the show.

SERVES 2

Here's what you'll need:

SALAD:

1 beet

2 carrots

1 Fuji apple

½ red onion

¼ cup sunflower seeds

¼ cup pumpkin seeds

½ red lettuce, chopped

½ romaine lettuce, chopped

2 bunches kale, leaves removed and chopped, stems discarded

½ cup crumbled feta cheese

Handful of fresh blueberries or raspberries

DRESSING:

2 garlic cloves, crushed

⅓ cup extra virgin olive oil

¼ cup balsamic vinegar

2 tablespoons maple syrup

1½ teaspoons kosher salt

Here's how it's done:

1. To prepare the salad, peel the beet with a paring knife or vegetable peeler, and grate with a food processor fitted with a shredding blade or a standard box grater with large-sized holes, then set aside. Peel and grate the carrots and set them aside. Leaving the skin on the apple, core it and dice into cubes. Add the apple to the beets, tossing lightly together. Thinly slice the onion. Add half to the beets and apple and half to the carrots.

2. In a dry skillet over high heat, toast the sunflower and pumpkin seeds until fragrant, about 3 to 4 minutes. Set aside to cool in a small bowl.

3. Place both lettuces and the kale on top of the beets and apples in the salad bowl—but don't toss just yet.

4. To make the dressing, in a jar, place the garlic, oil, balsamic, maple syrup, and salt. Shake well.

5. Now you can toss the ingredients in the salad bowl! Add your preferred amount of dressing and toss to distribute it evenly among the ingredients. Scatter the carrot and onion mixture and cheese overtop, toss once, and garnish with the berries as the crowning glory.

Perfect Greek Salad

When I lived in Banff, Alberta, one of my favorite things to do was go to the pool at the Banff Centre's fitness center and do some people watching while I sat by the pool and ate Greek salad. It felt so warm and tropical on winter days; the warmth and humidity offered by the pool coupled with a Mediterranean salad was always such a sharp contrast to the incredibly dry winter weather outside, with −40°C temperatures (which is equally as cold as −40°F—literally!) and snow as high as my knees. This salad keeps my memories of those days fresh in my mind.

SERVES 2–3

Here's what you'll need:

A Greek person to go shopping with . . .

A cold winter's day for inspiration . . .

OK, just kidding.

DRESSING:

4 cloves garlic, minced

1 cup extra virgin olive oil

2 lemons, 1 zested, both juiced

¼ cup red wine vinegar

2 teaspoons dried oregano

1 teaspoon dried basil

½ teaspoon dried thyme leaves

1 teaspoon granulated sugar

Kosher salt and ground black pepper

Small bunch fresh basil, for garnish

SALAD:

4 large field tomatoes, cut in wedges

1 large English cucumber, cubed

1 yellow bell pepper, cut into ½-inch-thick strips

1 red onion, thinly sliced

1 cup pitted Kalamata olives

¾ cup crumbled feta cheese

Here's how it's done:

1. The dressing for this salad becomes increasingly amazing the longer it sits, so feel free to whip it up even a couple of days ahead of time. To make the dressing, in a jar, combine the garlic, oil, lemon juice, and vinegar. Add the oregano, basil, and thyme. Shake to combine. Add the sugar and a pinch each of salt and fresh pepper. Give it another good shake.

2. To make the salad, in a salad bowl, toss together the tomatoes, cucumber, bell pepper, onion, and olives. Pour the dressing overtop, and add the lemon zest and cheese. Stir a couple of times to combine, and add a generous sprinkle of fresh basil and some more pepper to taste.

Buttermilk Dressing with Dill and Parsley

I used to have a cookbook that had been rendered dog-eared by use. The lodge staff and I practically loved it to death. One day, we discovered the page we needed was gone. This buttermilk dressing was my attempt to recreate the missing recipe—and it turned out to be creamier and yummier than the original!

MAKES 2 ¼ CUPS

Here's what you'll need:

¾ cup buttermilk

½ cup full-fat sour cream

2 tablespoons full-fat mayonnaise

1 tablespoon smooth Dijon mustard

½ teaspoon Worcestershire sauce

2 garlic cloves, minced

1 teaspoon liquid honey

Kosher salt and ground black pepper

2 tablespoons fresh flat-leaf or curly parsley

1 tablespoon chopped fresh chives

1 teaspoon dried tarragon

1 teaspoon dried dill

Here's how it's done:

1. In a mixing bowl, whisk together the buttermilk, sour cream, and mayonnaise. Add the Dijon and Worcestershire and whisk to combine. Add the garlic, honey, and salt and pepper to taste. Whisk very gently, just to combine—you're looking for creamy, not whipped.

2. Add the parsley, chives, tarragon, and dill. Stir gently to combine.

3. If you don't plan to use this immediately, don't add the parsley and chives until you're ready to serve. This dressing will keep, without the parsley and chives, in an airtight container in the fridge for up to 7 days.

Talus Backcountry Lodge

Having had the pleasure to work for and alongside owners Sara Renner and Thomas Grandi has been an absolute highlight of my backcountry career. Their patient, caring, and helpful attitude is infinitely present at Talus Backcountry Lodge and its surroundings.

Talus Backcountry Lodge is located in the outstanding Canadian Rockies, nestled in a spectacular alpine setting located on a limestone plateau between the upper reaches of the Cross and Albert Rivers and four kilometers (two and a half miles) south of Banff National Park's boundary. The area is a true wilderness, where a combination of streams, lakes, topography, and elevation offer the opportunity to experience nature and view wildlife from a very comfortable home base.

Operated by Sara and Thomas—mountain raised, Olympic skiers, and descendants of a long legacy of backcountry hospitality— Talus is a place to enjoy the simple pleasures of wilderness and backcountry skiing and hiking. You can venture off the beaten path with a Rocky Mountain snowpack to play in, larch-filled meadows to hike through, and peaks to hoot from. You can then return to the cozy lodge, with its fires blazing and hearty mountain food.

Simply put, Talus is a real journey for the soul, a pilgrimage to a special promise of unbounded kindness.

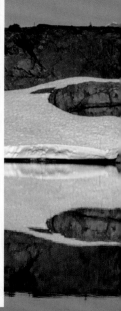

Meats and Fish

Fisherman's Ceviche

This recipe is a favorite for my husband and me because it brings back memories of our honeymoon in Belize. I'll never forget returning to the beach at Ambergris Quay, sunburned, salty, delirious, and starving, and seeing the fishing guide's wife waiting to meet us with a basket of goodies to prepare ceviche. The guide got busy preparing the fish, and his wife chopped up beautiful, vibrant fresh vegetables. I watched her put together a mouthwatering ceviche and then lay out a blanket on the cooling sand for us to savor our picnic and the setting sun. Total heaven.

SERVES 4–6

Here's what you'll need:

1¼ lb fresh fish (bass, halibut, snapper, trout, tuna), cleaned, filleted, and cut into ¼-inch cubes

1 red onion, thinly sliced

1 cup lime juice (about 8 limes)

¼ cup fresh orange juice (about 1 orange)

3 tomatoes, cut into ½-inch cubes

2 serrano or jalapeño chilies, deseeded and thinly sliced

2 garlic cloves, minced

½ cup coarsely chopped cilantro

Pink or kosher salt and ground black pepper

1 avocado, cubed

2 radishes, thinly sliced

¼ cup fresh mint leaves

7–10 oz fresh corn chips

Here's how it's done:

1. In a glass or other nonreactive mixing bowl, mix the fish with the onion. Pour the lime and orange juices over the fish and marinate for 15 to 20 minutes. If the fish is left too long, it begins to deteriorate and become somewhat pallid and chalky. It is important to use only fresh fish and to not marinate for longer than 1 hour.

2. While the fish is marinating, place the tomatoes, chilies, garlic, and cilantro in a large bowl and mix to combine. Drain the marinated fish in a colander, discarding the marinade, and add to the tomato mixture. Gently stir in a pinch each of salt and pepper. Add the avocado, radishes, and mint and mix to combine. Transfer to a serving dish and serve with corn chips on the side.

Baked Halibut with Scallops and Asparagus

Baked halibut is a summer staple at most lodges. Served with seared scallops on a bed of asparagus, it is a game changer. If you announce this menu on the trail, there will be a stampede back for supper! (Note that you will need two cast iron or stainless steel skillets for this recipe.)

SERVES 4

Here's what you'll need:

SCALLOPS:

1¼ lb fresh dry sea scallops

Kosher salt

1 tablespoon vegetable oil

HALIBUT:

3 tablespoons extra virgin olive oil

2 garlic cloves, minced

2 teaspoons grated lemon zest

1 teaspoon fresh thyme leaves

1 teaspoon dried dill

Kosher salt and ground black pepper

4 (6 oz, each about 1-inch thick) halibut fillets

ASPARAGUS:

1 lb fresh asparagus, ends trimmed

1 tablespoon extra virgin olive oil

Kosher salt and ground black pepper

Red pepper flakes

BEURRE BLANC:

½ cup dry white wine

¼ cup white wine vinegar

2 shallots, minced

1 garlic clove, minced

1 cup unsalted butter, cold, cut into tablespoon-size cubes

8–10 fresh basil leaves, chiffonade

1 tablespoon chopped fresh dill leaves

Here's how it's done:

1. Preheat the oven to 400°F. Grease a 13- × 9-inch baking sheet.

2. Place the scallops on some paper towel. Sprinkle just a pinch of salt overtop of each scallop—no need to overdo it. The salt will draw out any residual moisture, making for an extra-dry scallop that will sear well.

3. Prepare an herb rub for the halibut. In a shallow bowl, combine the oil, garlic, lemon zest, thyme, and dill. Add a pinch each of salt and pepper. Pat each fillet dry and lightly press the rub into the flesh on both sides. Place the fillets in the baking dish. Set aside.

4. To prepare the asparagus, place it on a separate, ungreased baking sheet and drizzle with the oil. Sprinkle on some salt and pepper and a pinch of red pepper flakes. Set aside.

5. Bake the halibut and asparagus for 10 minutes, or until the fillets have an internal temperature of 145°F.

6. In a cast iron or stainless steel skillet over high heat, warm the 1 tablespoon of vegetable oil for 1 full minute until very hot. Add the scallops and let cook until there is a heavenly golden crust on the pan side. This should take 1½ to 2 minutes. Flip and repeat on the second side. Remove the scallops from the pan and set aside.

7. To make the beurre blanc, heat a clean cast iron or stainless steel skillet over medium-high heat. Add the wine and vinegar, followed by the shallots and garlic. Stir to combine and bring to a gentle boil. Turn down the heat to medium-low and let reduce for about 5 minutes. It will reduce to almost nothing, about 2 tablespoons.

8. Turn down the heat to low and begin adding the butter, one cube at time, reserving two cubes. Keep the butter moving and allow each cube to melt before you add the next one. The butter should melt gently and the pan should not get so hot that the sauce separates. Remove the pan from the heat and let stand for 1 minute. Now stir in the final two pieces of cold butter. At this point, the sauce should be thick and creamy. For a velvety sauce, press the beurre blanc through a sieve to capture the shallots and garlic.

9. Divide the asparagus between each plate and set the halibut overtop. Place the scallops around the halibut and top generously with the warm beurre blanc. Garnish each plate with fresh basil and dill.

Halibut Tacos

Use this recipe to jazz up a weeknight dinner or turn any weekend get-together into a party. It's a lot of fun to prepare all of the components ahead of time and then invite your friends and family to partake in building their own tacos with all the delicious ingredients.

SERVES 6

Here's what you'll need:

HALIBUT:

2 tablespoons white miso paste

6 tablespoons lemon juice (about 2 lemons)

2 tablespoons vegetable oil

1 garlic clove, crushed

1 tablespoon granulated sugar

1 tablespoon liquid honey or agave nectar

1 teaspoon kosher salt

2 tablespoons extra virgin olive oil

2 tablespoons salted butter

1½–2 lb fresh halibut, filleted and cut into 1-inch strips

20–24 medium prawns, peeled and deveined

AIOLI:

2 garlic cloves, crushed

1½ cups full-fat mayonnaise

½ cup lemon juice (about 2 large lemons)

2 tablespoons sriracha

1 tablespoon ground cumin

1 tablespoon paprika (any type)

1 teaspoon ground coriander

1 tablespoon granulated sugar

Kosher salt

TACOS:

12 (each 6-inch) corn tortillas

3 cups grated white cheddar cheese

1 romaine lettuce, shredded

1 tomato, diced

1 white onion, diced

1 avocado, pitted and sliced

1 bunch cilantro, roughly chopped

1 lemon (optional)

Here's how it's done:

1. Preheat the oven to 350°F.

2. Place the miso, lemon juice, and vegetable oil in a mixing bowl and whisk gently so it doesn't splatter. Add the garlic, sugar, honey, and salt. Whisk to combine and set aside.

3. In a large skillet over medium heat, warm the olive oil and butter until the butter has melted. Add the halibut and fry for about 3 to 4 minutes, turning it a couple of times, to par-cook. Add the miso mixture and, using a wooden spoon, mix into the cooking liquid. Add the prawns and sauté until the halibut is cooked through and the prawns are opaque and starting to curl on themselves, about 4 minutes. Remove from the pan and transfer to a serving platter, making sure to scrape any larger bits off the bottom of the skillet. Set aside.

4. To make the aioli, in a medium bowl, whisk together the garlic, mayonnaise, lemon juice, and sriracha until well blended. Add the cumin, paprika, and coriander. Whisk to combine. Finally, add the sugar and a pinch of salt, mix again, and set aside.

5. To prepare the tacos, wrap the tortillas in batches of six in aluminum foil and place in the oven for 15 to 20 minutes, or until heated through.

6. Place the halibut and prawns in a small serving dish. Add the cheese, lettuce, tomato, onion, avocado, and cilantro on a large serving platter or in separate serving bowls. Set out tongs alongside the platter or bowls and spritz a bit of lemon onto the avocado if you are not planning on serving immediately, to keep it from browning.

7. To assemble, stuff the warm tortilla shells with the halibut and prawns, cheese, lettuce, tomatoes, onion, and avocado. Drizzle as much aioli as you like on to the whole thing and top with a generous handful of cilantro.

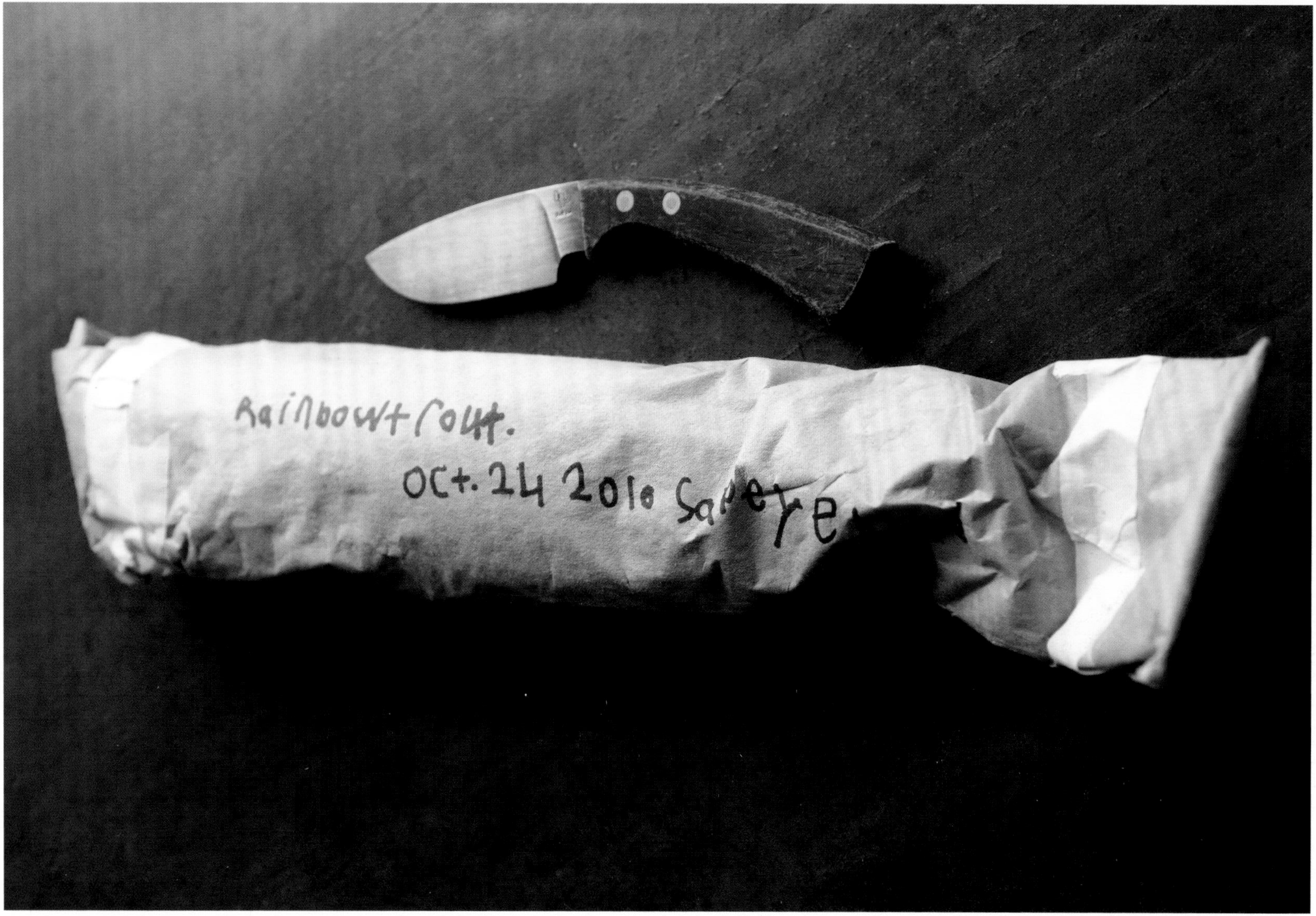
Rainbow trout.
Oct. 24 2010 Sapere.

Red Deer Lake Trout with Lemon and Bugaboos Honey

Backcountry lodges attract a lot of fishing enthusiasts; they love the remoteness of so many of the lakes and the breathtaking landscapes. I am often presented with beautiful, freshly caught fish at the door to the kitchen. This recipe is a simple yet sensational way to honor the fish.

SERVES 4–6

Here's what you'll need:

1 (2–3 lb) whole lake trout, cleaned and butterflied

½ cup salted butter

3 garlic cloves, cut into rounds

1 tablespoon lemon juice

1 teaspoon grated lemon zest

2 tablespoons smooth Dijon mustard

2 tablespoons liquid honey

1 tablespoon fresh dill fronds

Kosher salt and ground black pepper

1 lemon, cut into rounds

½ white onion, thinly sliced

Here's how it's done:

1. Preheat the oven to 400°F.

2. Using warm water, rinse the fish and pat dry with paper towel. Drying it will prevent the fish from steaming in the oven. Take a large baking sheet and place a piece of aluminum foil twice its length in the center of it. Place a sheet of parchment paper in the center of the foil. Place the whole fish on the parchment.

3. In a saucepan over medium heat, melt the butter. Add the garlic and sauté until soft, about 3 minutes. Add the lemon juice and zest, Dijon, and honey. Whisk together, turn down the heat to low, and gently warm for 3 more minutes.

4. Pour the honey mixture over and inside the butterflied fish, and then sprinkle the dill and salt and pepper to taste inside and out. Place half of the lemon and onion inside the fish and half on the outside, on the top of the fish skin.

5. Wrap the fish in the foil, cinching the seam tightly to make sure there are no gaps. Bake on the middle rack of the oven for 20 minutes for a 2 to 3 lb fish (about 15 minutes for a smaller one).

6. Remove the baking sheet, fold back the foil to reveal the fish, and return it to the oven for 10 to 14 minutes (5 to 9 minutes for a smaller fish). This will allow the skin to get a bit of a crunch and crackle to it. The fish is done when it is an opaque white and has a flaky texture. The internal temperature should be 145°F.

7. Remove the fish from the oven and slide onto a serving platter. Drizzle with the sauce that is inside the foil pouch and serve with a large fork and fish turner. Make sure everyone watches for bones.

Teriyaki Salmon

This salmon recipe has been with me for so long that I can't recall when I first had it or made it, or a time when I didn't know about it. It is such a staple in my lodge repertoire that I almost take it for granted. If you need a super-quick dinner that's also healthy and bursting with flavor, this might be your new go-to.

SERVES 4

Here's what you'll need:

TERIYAKI SAUCE:

½ cup soy sauce

½ cup packed brown sugar

2 tablespoons rice wine vinegar

2 tablespoons balsamic vinegar

2–3 garlic cloves, minced

1-inch piece ginger, peeled and grated

½ teaspoon red pepper flakes

½ teaspoon sesame seeds (any color)

2 tablespoons cornstarch

SALMON:

4 (each 6 oz) salmon fillets

Kosher salt and ground black pepper

Here's how it's done:

1. Lightly oil a baking dish just large enough to hold the fish without crowding.

2. To make the teriyaki sauce, in a saucepan over medium heat, warm the soy sauce with the sugar. Whisk well to combine. Add ½ cup of water and both vinegars, and whisk to combine. Add the garlic, ginger, red pepper flakes, and sesame seeds. Whisking continuously to avoid sticking, bring to a boil. Continue to whisk gently for 1 full minute. Turn down the heat to low and let the sauce simmer for a minute or two while you prepare the cornstarch and water mixture (in the next Step).

3. Dissolve the cornstarch in ¼ cup of cold water. Add this to the sauce and whisk well. Turn up the heat to medium-high and simmer for 2 minutes. Turn down the heat to low, whisking occasionally to keep the sauce blended nicely, for 5 more minutes, to continue thickening. Taste for seasoning. Remove from the heat and set aside when the desired consistency and flavors are reached. The sauce can be stored in an airtight container in the fridge for 2 weeks.

4. Preheat the oven to 400°F.

5. To prepare the salmon, pat it dry and lightly season with salt and pepper. Place each piece of salmon skin side down in the baking dish. Bake for 6 minutes. Remove from the oven and pour 1 to 2 tablespoons of the teriyaki sauce over the salmon. Return the salmon to the oven for another 6 to 8 minutes, or until it flakes easily when scraped with a fork and the internal temperature at the thickest part of the fillet is 145°F.

6. Plate the salmon fillets and drizzle with the remaining teriyaki sauce.

Grilled Backcountry Prawns with Brava Sauce

When I'm preparing meals in the backcountry, I really enjoy having a staple like this piquant, classic sauce to elevate my game. This recipe comes complete with grilled prawns on skewers to accompany the spicy, smoky tomato dipping sauce.

SERVES 4

Here's what you'll need:

BRAVA SAUCE:

3 tablespoons extra virgin olive oil

½ cup white onion, diced

3 garlic cloves, minced

1 (14.5 oz) can diced tomatoes

1 roasted red bell pepper, chopped

2 tablespoons sherry vinegar

2 teaspoons granulated sugar

1½ teaspoons smoked paprika

1 teaspoon chili powder

Cayenne pepper

1 tablespoon full-fat mayonnaise

PRAWNS:

1 garlic clove, crushed

1 teaspoon paprika (any type)

Kosher salt

2 teaspoons lemon juice

2 tablespoons extra virgin olive oil

½ teaspoon hot sauce

2 lb large prawns or shrimp, peeled and deveined

Here's how it's done:

1. To make the sauce, in a saucepan over medium heat, warm the olive oil. Add the onion and garlic and sauté until the onion begins to soften and the garlic is increasingly aromatic, about 5 to 6 minutes.

2. Stir in the tomatoes with their juice, the bell pepper, vinegar, sugar, paprika, chili powder, and a pinch of cayenne pepper. Turn down the heat to medium-low and let simmer, uncovered, until thickened, about 20 minutes.

3. Remove from the heat and let cool before puréeing. (At this point, if you're planning to use bamboo skewers to cook the prawns, drop them into water to begin soaking.)

4. Using a blender or immersion blender, purée the sauce until smooth. If using an immersion blender, make sure you are wearing an apron. Add the mayonnaise and give it one more good spin. Adjust seasoning to taste.

5. Once your brava is bravo, you can head on out to the barbecue and heat it to medium.

6. To prepare the prawns, in a bowl, mix together the garlic, paprika, and a pinch of salt. Add the lemon juice and stir to make a paste. Slowly whisk in the olive oil and hot sauce. Toss the prawns in this light marinade to coat.

7. Start threading the prawns onto the skewers, starting at the thickest part and finishing with the tail, essentially making a "C" shape. Aim for five prawns per skewer. For juicier prawns, place them close together; for a more grilled effect, place them further apart.

8. Lightly oil the grill. Grill the prawns for 2 to 3 minutes per side, or until they turn pink on the outside and are white all the way through on the inside.

9. Serve with the homemade brava sauce.

Wild Chimichurri for Grilled Meats

Chimichurri is an uncooked sauce perfect for grilled meats, fish, and wild game. This recipe combines the joys of grilling with the tastes of the outdoors. I hope you will feel inspired to bring it along on your next backpacking adventure. It also doubles well, if you're serving a crowd.

MAKES ABOUT 1 CUP

Here's what you'll need:

½ cup white wine vinegar

2 tablespoons white miso paste

3 garlic cloves, quartered

¼ cup roughly chopped fresh flat-leaf parsley

¼ cup roughly chopped fresh cilantro

¼ cup fresh basil leaves

2 tablespoons fresh oregano leaves

1–2 teaspoons crushed red pepper flakes

Kosher salt and ground black pepper

⅔ cup extra virgin olive oil

Here's how it's done:

1. In a food processor, combine the vinegar, miso, and 2 tablespoons of water with the garlic, parsley, cilantro, basil, oregano, and red pepper flakes. Process until mostly smooth but still a teeny bit coarse. Add a pinch each of salt and pepper and pulse to combine. With the machine running, drizzle in the oil. Turn off the food processor as soon as the oil is incorporated.

2. It is always a good idea to make your chimichurri at least 30 minutes before using it so the herbs and spices can get to know each other.

NOTE: Chimichurri stores well in the refrigerator for 2 weeks; the acids in the vinegar keeps the herbs bright and fresh. Make sure to remove it from the fridge 30 minutes before use, to allow it get back to room temperature.

Mountain Pork Medallions with Hinterland Mushrooms

Pork tenderloin paired with a cream sauce is a legendary combination and a classic for a reason. The spice rub in this recipe only enhances an already amazing pairing and gives a smoky, earthy flavor to the finished product.

SERVES 4

Here's what you'll need:

PORK:

2 (each 1–1½ lb) pork tenderloins

RUB:

½ cup packed brown sugar

¼ cup granulated sugar

2 teaspoons ground black pepper

1 teaspoon kosher salt

2 teaspoons ground ginger

2 teaspoons garlic powder

2 teaspoons onion salt

2 teaspoons dried mustard

1 teaspoon Spanish paprika

1 teaspoon ground cumin

1 teaspoon ground coriander

½ teaspoon dried thyme leaves

CREAM SAUCE:

3 tablespoons salted butter, divided

1 tablespoon extra virgin olive oil

½ lb cremini mushrooms, wiped and quartered

2 shallots, diced

¼ cup white wine

¼ cup cognac or brandy

½ cup chicken stock

1 cup full-fat sour cream

½ cup whipping (35%) cream

2 rosemary sprigs, chopped

3 green onions, chopped, for garnish

Here's how it's done:

1. Trim off any excess fat and silver skin from the pork. Pat dry and set aside.

2. In a shallow dish, combine both sugars with the pepper and salt. Add the ginger, garlic powder, onion salt, mustard, paprika, cumin, coriander, and thyme and mix to combine. Set aside.

3. Liberally coat the tenderloin with the spice rub, ensuring the rub adheres to the pork's surface. You don't need an extra-thick coating. Place the pork on a plate and set aside. Discard any unused spice rub.

4. Preheat the oven to 450°F. Lightly oil a 13- × 9-inch baking dish.

5. To make the sauce, in a cast iron skillet over medium-high heat, warm 2 tablespoons of the butter and the oil. Add the mushrooms and sauté. Once they start to brown, add the shallots. Sauté until the mushrooms are browned and the shallots are softened, about 5 minutes. Remove from the pan and set aside.

6. Keeping the pan on medium-high heat, add the tenderloins, one at a time. Sear each side for 2 minutes. Transfer to the prepared baking dish. Bake for 15 minutes, turn once, and bake for 5 more minutes. Remove from the oven when the internal temperature is 160°F in the thickest part.

7. Meanwhile, add the white wine and cognac to the hot skillet. Scrape the bottom of the skillet to lift any rub and seared pork bits, plus the sticky bits from the sugars. Add the stock and reduce over medium heat for about 8 to 10 minutes. Remove from the heat and whisk in both creams vigorously until incorporated. Return to the stovetop and simmer over medium-low heat. Add the rosemary and reduce for 15 minutes, or until the sauce coats the back of a wooden spoon.

8. Let the cooked tenderloins rest for about 10 minutes in the baking dish, then transfer to a cutting board. Using a very sharp knife, cut each into ½-inch-thick medallions.

9. Place the medallions on a serving platter in two equal rows. Top with the mushrooms and shallots and finish with the cream sauce overtop. Garnish with the green onions.

Lodge-Perfect Pork Chops

These pork chops are always a hit with hungry folks. This recipe combines a juicy, bone-in pork chop with a flavorful yogurt sauce to knock it right out of the backcountry. When choosing pork chops, look for a pinkish-red color and some marbling of the meat throughout.

SERVES 4

Here's what you'll need:

PORK CHOPS:

4 (each ¾-inch-thick) bone-in pork chops

1 cup all-purpose flour

2 tablespoons cornstarch

1 teaspoon kosher salt

1 teaspoon ground black pepper

1 teaspoon garlic powder

1 teaspoon onion powder

1 teaspoon paprika (any type)

½ teaspoon cayenne pepper

⅔ cup vegetable oil

YOGURT SAUCE:

¾ cup Greek yogurt

2 tablespoons white wine vinegar

2 teaspoons extra virgin olive oil

2 garlic cloves, crushed

2 teaspoons dried dill or 1 tablespoon
    chopped fresh dill leaves

1 teaspoon dried oregano

Kosher salt and ground black pepper

Here's how it's done:

1. Remove the pork chops from the fridge and let sit at room temperature for about 30 to 40 minutes. Pat dry and set aside on a plate.

2. To make the yogurt sauce, in a mixing bowl, whisk together the yogurt, vinegar, and oil. Mix in the garlic, followed by the dill, oregano, and a pinch each of salt and pepper. Set aside, covered, at room temperature.

3. To prepare the chops, combine the flour, cornstarch, salt, pepper, garlic powder, onion powder, paprika, and cayenne in a large mixing bowl.

4. Dredge each pork chop through this rub, pressing down so that it adheres. Shake off the excess and place the chops on a dry plate.

5. In a large skillet over high heat, warm the vegetable oil. Cook the chops, two at a time so as not to crowd the pan, for 4 to 5 minutes per side, until the internal temperature at the thickest part, not touching bone, is 145°F. Place the cooked chops on a wire rack set over a baking sheet to drain off any accumulated oil. Place a sheet of aluminum foil overtop to keep them warm while you cook the other two.

6. Plate the chops and serve with a dollop of yogurt sauce on the side. Set the rest aside in a small serving bowl for seconds. If there are any leftovers, you can store them in an airtight container for 2 or 3 days. These pork chops are a sure hit served with First Tracks Salad (page 131).

Pan-Seared Beef Tenderloin with Peppercorn Gravy

My in-laws are cattle ranchers, and I cannot recall a year when we haven't been dazzled by their amazing, farm-raised cows. In all the time that I have been fortunate enough to eat their beef, I have been consistently thrilled by how little attention this organic meat needs. This recipe takes nothing away from the meat, allowing it to be simple yet complex in its textures and richness. If you don't have a ranch at your disposal, you can find wonderful cuts of beef tenderloin at your nearest butcher or grocery store.

SERVES 4

Here's what you'll need:

TENDERLOIN:

4 (each 8–10 oz) tenderloin fillets

Kosher salt and ground black pepper

¼ cup salted butter

2 tablespoons grapeseed oil

PEPPERCORN GRAVY:

1 tablespoon salted butter

3 tablespoons green peppercorns in brine, drained

3 teaspoons cracked black peppercorns

2 garlic cloves, minced

1 cup beef stock

3 tablespoons dry red wine

1 tablespoon port or sherry

¼ cup whipping (35–40%) cream

2 thyme sprigs

Kosher salt

Worcestershire sauce

Here's how it's done:

1. Preheat the oven to 425°F.

2. Pat the tenderloins dry and generously season with salt and pepper.

3. In a cast iron skillet over high heat (I mean, raging hot), melt the butter with the oil. Make sure you have an apron on for this, as the grease will spit when you add your fillets. Sear each tenderloin for 2 minutes per side. Wearing good-quality oven mitts, transfer the skillet to the oven. Cook in the oven for 5 to 6 minutes, or until the internal temperature is 145°F, or slightly lower for medium-rare. Remove to a warm plate and lightly tent with aluminum foil.

4. To make the gravy, place the skillet (it will still be warm, so be careful) over medium heat and melt the butter. Add the green and cracked black peppercorns. Using a wooden spoon, stir in the minced garlic and sauté for 1 minute. Pour in the stock, wine, and port. Whisk to blend and bring to a boil. Turn down the heat to low and simmer for about 5 to 6 minutes, until it has started to thicken and the yummy bits are lifting off the bottom of the skillet.

5. Remove from the heat and whisk in the cream, thyme, and a pinch of salt. Return to the heat to simmer on low for another 5 minutes, or until the sauce coats the back of a wooden spoon. Add a dash of Worcestershire and give it all one final stir.

6. Plate the fillets. Pour any drippings from the platter into the skillet with the gravy and give it a quick whisk. Spoon the creamy peppercorn gravy over the tenderloin fillets and serve immediately.

Seasonal Lamb with Mint Relish

Lamb offers a flavor experience like no other, and this amazing marinade not only enhances the natural taste but also creates a fall-off-the bone tenderness. (Note that you have to prep this the night before you plan to eat it.)

SERVES 4–5

Here's what you'll need:

LAMB:

¼ cup extra virgin olive oil

¾ cup rice wine vinegar

¼ cup dry red wine

¼ cup soy sauce

1 tablespoon smooth Dijon mustard

½ teaspoon fennel seeds

½ teaspoon caraway seeds

½ teaspoon mustard seeds (yellow or black)

1 medium shallot, chopped

2 tablespoons chopped fresh mint leaves

1 tablespoon dried mint

1 tablespoon chopped fresh rosemary leaves

4 garlic cloves, minced

½ cup packed dark brown sugar

8–10 (each 3 oz) lamb chops, about ¾-inch thick

MINT RELISH:

½ cup roughly chopped fresh flat-leaf parsley

½ cup roughly chopped mint leaves

¼ cup roughly chopped cilantro

¼ cup chopped fresh chives

½ cup white wine vinegar

2 tablespoons granulated sugar

1-inch piece ginger, peeled

3 garlic cloves, minced

2 tablespoons white miso paste

2 tablespoons fresh oregano leaves

1 teaspoon red pepper flakes

Kosher salt and ground black pepper

¾ cup extra virgin olive oil

Here's how it's done:

1. To prepare the lamb, in a mixing bowl, whisk together the oil, vinegar, wine, soy sauce, and Dijon. Whisk in the fennel, caraway, and mustard seeds, followed by the shallot, fresh and dried mint, and rosemary. Add the garlic and sugar and whisk to combine. Transfer to a plastic resealable bag.

2. Trim any excess fat off the lamb chops and place them in the marinade, turning them over a few times to coat well. Refrigerate overnight.

3. The next day, remove the marinated lamb from the fridge at least 1 hour before you plan to cook it.

4. Preheat the oven to 375°F. Line a baking sheet with parchment paper.

5. To make the mint relish, place the parsley, mint, cilantro, and chives in a food processor and pulse to combine. Add the vinegar and sugar and pulse to blend. Grate the ginger right into the sauce and then add the garlic, miso, oregano, red pepper flakes, a pinch or two of salt, and pepper to taste. Pulse a few times to combine, drizzling in the olive oil as you do so. Continue to pulse just until you have a chunky and wonderfully textured sauce. It should be almost pourable but not runny. Transfer the sauce to a bowl and set aside. You can also prepare this relish ahead of time and keep it in the fridge.

6. Remove the lamb chops from the marinade, one at a time, allowing any excess liquid to drip off. Place them on the prepared baking sheet. Cook in the oven for 12 to 15 minutes. For medium-rare, the internal temperature should read about 130°F. It is best to remove the chops when just shy of this temperature, because they will continue cooking after you remove them.

7. Plate the lamb and serve with a dollop of mint relish.

8. If you have any leftover relish, you can store it in an airtight container in the refrigerator for 1 week. You will need to remove it from the refrigerator about 30 minutes before using, to allow the oil to come back up to room temperature after solidifying. Just give it a gentle stir before using.

Savory Aioli Chicken

Don't be surprised if you find yourself dreaming about this chicken recipe, with its aromatic and piquant aioli. The number of requests I get for this at the lodge has me convinced that a lot of folks are thinking about it when they're not actually eating it. Now you can make it a weekly addition to your dinner table. The aioli is also a great spread to keep in the fridge.

SERVES 6

Here's what you'll need:

CHICKEN:

½ cup extra virgin olive oil

¼ cup lemon juice (1–2 lemons)

Zest of 1 large lemon

1 tablespoon ground cumin

1 tablespoon paprika (any type)

1 tablespoon garlic salt

2 teaspoons kosher salt

2 teaspoons granulated sugar

1 tablespoon sriracha

6 boneless, skinless chicken breasts

1 lemon, cut into wedges

AIOLI:

1 cup full-fat mayonnaise

½ cup lemon juice (about 3 lemons)

2 tablespoons sriracha

2 garlic cloves, minced

2 tablespoons fresh cilantro

1 tablespoon granulated sugar

2 teaspoons ground cumin

2 teaspoons paprika (any type)

1 teaspoon ground coriander

Kosher salt

Here's how it's done:

1. To prepare the chicken, in a deep baking dish or large mixing bowl, whisk together the oil, lemon juice and zest, cumin, paprika, garlic salt, kosher salt, sugar, and sriracha.

2. Place the chicken breasts in the marinade and toss to coat evenly. You can leave them in the mixing bowl or transfer everything to a resealable plastic bag. Either way, refrigerate them for at least 4 hours, or up to 24 hours.

3. Preheat the oven to 400°F. Lightly oil a 13- × 9-inch baking dish.

4. Remove the chicken breasts from the marinade, shaking off any excess, and place them in the prepared baking dish. Tuck a couple of lemon wedges around the chicken. Cover the chicken completely with parchment paper, making sure to press the parchment down in the corners so nothing is peeking out.

5. Bake on the middle rack of the oven for 35 to 40 minutes, or until an instant-read thermometer reads 165°F inserted into the thickest part of the breast. This cooking method ensures the juiciest chicken breasts.

6. Meanwhile, make the aioli. (It can also be prepared in advance and stored in an airtight container in the fridge for up to 2 weeks.)

7. In a small bowl, whisk together the mayonnaise, lemon juice, and sriracha to combine well. Add the garlic, cilantro, sugar, cumin, paprika, coriander, and a pinch or two of salt. Whisk until the aioli becomes a solid salmon color and there are no clumps of seasoning. At this point you can adjust the seasoning to taste.

8. Once the chicken is done and the aioli is perfection itself, transfer the chicken to a serving platter and spoon the aioli overtop.

Fried Chicken

This crispy, juicy, fried chicken is a finger-licking sensation for any occasion. It tastes amazing with buttermilk dipping sauce—whether hot or cold, as an evening meal or sitting out by a lake on a summer afternoon.

SERVES 4

Here's what you'll need:

1 (about 2½ lb) whole chicken, skin on

2 tablespoons apple cider vinegar

2 tablespoons kosher salt

1 tablespoon granulated sugar

1 tablespoon mustard seeds (yellow or black)

2 teaspoons garlic powder

2 teaspoons onion powder

1 teaspoon ground black pepper

1 teaspoon cayenne pepper (optional)

1 cup all-purpose flour

4 cups vegetable oil

1 cup bacon fat or lard

Buttermilk sauce (page 138), for dipping

Here's how it's done:

1. Cut the chicken into eight pieces and place it in a large bowl or saucepan. Combine the vinegar, salt, sugar, and mustard seeds with 10 cups of water and pour over the chicken. Cover and refrigerate overnight.

2. In a mixing bowl, combine the garlic powder, onion powder, black pepper, and cayenne pepper (if using).

3. Remove the chicken from the brine about 30 to 40 minutes prior to frying. Pat dry and sprinkle with about half of the seasoning mixture. Place the remaining seasoning and the flour in a heavy plastic bag. Add one or two chicken pieces and shake the bag well. Start with the larger pieces so you can get them cooking in the hot oil.

4. In a heavy-bottomed saucepan or Dutch oven over medium-high heat, warm the oil and bacon fat. (It needs to be deep enough to cover the chicken.) It should register 350°F on a candy thermometer. If you don't have an oil or candy thermometer, simply place a wooden spoon, handle down, in the hot oil. If bubbles form around the handle where it meets the oil and the oil is also rippling slightly, you are good to go.

5. Working in batches so as not to overcrowd your saucepan, cook the chicken pieces for 6 minutes with the saucepan covered and then 9 minutes uncovered. Turn the chicken with tongs and cook for another 6 minutes covered, and 9 minutes uncovered. This may seem obsessive, but the covered and uncovered timings make a huge difference to the final product. When cooked, the internal temperature of the chicken should be 165°F.

6. Set the cooked chicken on a wire rack set over a baking sheet to catch excess oil for a couple of minutes. Tent the cooked chicken in aluminum foil on a separate baking sheet and place in a warm oven (about 165°F) while the remainder of the chicken is being prepared.

7. Enjoy this with your family and friends—don't forget the buttermilk sauce for dipping!

Sides and Satisfiers

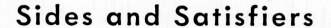

BBQ Corn on the Cob with Herbed Béchamel

This recipe brings back so many memories of summer corn roasts when I was a kid. We used to go to the local farms and find the best of the best corn—we all became obsessive and competitive running around the maze of a cornfield, searching for the ideal contenders. With this herbed béchamel, though, every piece of corn is a winner.

SERVES 6

Here's what you'll need:

CORN:

1 tablespoon kosher salt

6 ears corn on the cob

SAUCE:

3 cups 2% milk

1 cup whipping (35–40%) cream

5 tablespoons salted butter

4 tablespoons all-purpose flour

2 teaspoons kosher salt

3 green onions, chopped

2 tablespoons chopped fresh dill leaves

2 tablespoons chopped fresh chives

2 tablespoons chopped fresh flat-leaf parsley

Ground black pepper

Here's how it's done:

1. Fill a large saucepan with cold water and add the salt. Peel back the husks of each corn cob, keeping them intact, and remove as much of the silk as possible. Bundle the husks back up around the corn and place each cob in the cold water. Soak for 30 minutes—or no longer than 1 hour. This ensures the corn remains moist and the husks soften when barbecuing.

2. Remove the corn from the water and shake off any excess.

3. Preheat the barbecue to medium-high heat, about 400°F.

4. Place the corn on the grill and cook for 20 to 25 minutes, turning about every 5 minutes for even cooking, until the kernels are fork-tender and the husks are getting cool grill marks.

5. While the corn is cooking, prepare the sauce. In a saucepan, gently warm—but don't boil—the milk and cream. This will prevent them from splitting.

6. Melt the butter in a separate saucepan on medium heat. Add the flour and mix until a paste forms. This is called a roux.

7. Add the warm milk and cream combo to the roux, ½ cup at a time, whisking constantly to incorporate. Add the salt, continuing to whisk vigorously to get rid of any lumps.

8. Fold in the green onions, dill, chives, parsley, and pepper to taste.

9. Remove the corn from the barbecue and discard the husks. You can either drop the corn into the sauce and remove it with the tongs, or transfer it to a plate and pour the cream sauce.

Butternut Squash and Fennel

Backcountry lodge kitchens are always bustling in the high season. There are endless days of hungry hikers and skiers, and sometimes the vegetable pantry looks almost barren while we wait for the next food order to find its way out to us. But as crazy as it sounds, this is when the cooking can get fun! I get to be creative and innovative as I see what I can come up with that is both hearty and healthy, and plays well with whatever other ingredients I have on hand. This recipe is one such example.

SERVES 4

Here's what you'll need:

1 (about 2–3 lb) butternut squash

2 fennel bulbs

2 tablespoons extra virgin olive oil, divided

Kosher salt and ground black pepper

½ white onion, sliced

2 garlic cloves, minced

1 cup grated Gruyère cheese

Here's how it's done:

1. Preheat the oven to 375°F.

2. Use a vegetable peeler to remove the outer skin of the butternut squash. Leave the smooth surface under the peel intact. Cut off the stem and bottom ends, and then cut the squash in half across its narrowest point. Scoop out and discard the seeds. Cut the squash horizontally into slices about ½-inch thick. Place them in a mixing bowl.

3. Cut off the frond ends of the fennel, saving about 2 tablespoons of the fronds. Cut the root end off and discard the outer layer. Now cut vertically to make long slices about ½-inch thick. Place the cut fennel in the bowl with the squash.

4. Add 1 tablespoon of the oil and a generous pinch each of salt and pepper to the vegetables and toss. Add the onion, another ½ tablespoon of the oil, and the garlic, and toss again. Place the remaining ½ tablespoon of oil in a 13- × 9-inch baking dish and wipe it around with paper towel. Pour in the vegetable mixture. Add a pinch more salt and pepper and roast for 35 to 40 minutes, until the squash is fork-tender.

5. Remove from the oven and scatter the cheese evenly overtop. Return to the oven for another 10 minutes to allow the cheese to melt.

6. Sprinkle the reserved green, leafy fronds overtop for a wonderful and fresh finish.

Wild Rice and Quinoa
with Cumin Vinaigrette

Lodge life can sometimes mean long shifts and long days interspersed with incredible, gourmet backcountry meals. When you are working these kinds of days and feeling overwhelmed by the richness and flavors of the food, it is occasionally nice to dig into a smaller, more casual meal.

SERVES 4

Here's what you'll need:

RICE BLEND:

⅓ cup whole-grain brown basmati rice

¼ cup long-grain wild rice

⅓ cup uncooked quinoa

⅓ cup red lentils

2½ cups chicken stock

2 tablespoons salted butter

CUMIN VINAIGRETTE:

2 garlic cloves, minced

⅓ cup rice wine vinegar

2 teaspoons granulated sugar

1½ teaspoons ground cumin

1 teaspoon smooth Dijon mustard

Kosher salt and ground black pepper

½ teaspoon ground cinnamon

½ teaspoon ground cloves

½ teaspoon ground ginger

½ teaspoon ground cardamom

½ teaspoon ground coriander

½ teaspoon paprika (any type)

½ teaspoon ground turmeric

¼ teaspoon cayenne pepper

¼ cup canola oil

1 (13.5 oz) can full-fat coconut milk, very cold, stirred

Fresh flat-leaf parsley and cilantro, for garnish

Here's how it's done:

1. Rinse the quinoa in a sieve and shake off any excess water.

2. To make the rice blend, place both types of rice, the quinoa, and lentils in a saucepan over medium-high heat. Add the stock and butter, mix to combine, and bring to a boil. Boil, uncovered, for 5 minutes. Turn down the heat to low, cover with a tight-fitting lid, and simmer for another 30 to 35 minutes. Remove from the heat and let stand, covered, for 5 to 10 minutes.

3. While the rice blend is cooking, prepare the vinaigrette. In a mixing bowl, whisk together the garlic, vinegar, sugar, cumin, Dijon, and salt and pepper to taste. Add the cinnamon, cloves, ginger, cardamom, coriander, paprika, turmeric, and cayenne and whisk well to combine. Gradually whisk in the oil to ensure it emulsifies smoothly.

4. Carefully pour this mixture over the cooked rice blend. You don't need to use the entire amount if you feel it is too much.

5. Plate the rice blend on individual serving dishes. Open the can of cold coconut milk and carefully add a large spoonful of the solidified coconut milk to each serving. Store the remaining coconut milk in an airtight container for another use. The coconut milk will begin to melt and add a wonderful presentation as well as a creamy texture. Sprinkle parsley and cilantro overtop to finish.

Roast Carrots in a Spicy Glaze

Sometimes it is nice to have a veggie dish to fall back on when you have been out skiing all day and you have company coming for dinner! This recipe is one that you'll be able to pull together lickety-split. Having a small selection of condiments in the fridge can make or break the menu for a dinner party—especially one you start hosting in your ski socks.

SERVES 4

Here's what you'll need:

CARROTS:

6–8 carrots

1½ tablespoons vegetable oil

Kosher salt and ground black pepper

GLAZE:

2 garlic cloves, minced

2 tablespoons liquid honey

1 tablespoon sambal oelek

2 teaspoons salted butter, melted

Here's how it's done:

1. Preheat the oven to 350°F.

2. To prepare the carrots, peel them and cut into your preferred shape. I prefer the baton cut, which is basically your everyday carrot stick. You can even trim off the rounded edges for the perfect look. The important thing is to make the pieces the same size and length so that they cook evenly. Place the carrots on the baking tray. Drizzle the oil overtop and season lightly with salt and pepper.

3. Roast for 35 to 40 minutes, turning often. Transfer the carrots to a serving dish.

4. To make the glaze, in a saucepan over low heat, mix together the garlic, honey, sambal oelek, and butter and heat for 1 to 2 minutes. Pour slowly over the cooked carrots and serve immediately.

Smashed Potatoes

This recipe is a playful spin on the classic roast potato. Smashed potatoes look fun and enticing on the plate and pair wonderfully with any main dish; they're also delicious on their own with a side of brava sauce (page 153). If you are looking for a new and creative potato recipe, this might just become your new favorite.

SERVES 4

Here's what you'll need:

2 lb multi-colored baby potatoes

3 tablespoons extra virgin olive oil, divided

2 tablespoons salted butter, cubed very small

10 thyme sprigs, halved

Kosher salt and ground black pepper

¾ cup grated Parmigiano-Reggiano cheese

¼ teaspoon paprika (any type) (optional)

Here's how it's done:

1. Preheat the oven to 450°F.

2. Place the whole, clean potatoes in a 13- × 9-inch baking dish. Pour ¾ cup of water into the dish and cover with aluminum foil. Bake on the middle rack of the oven for 20 minutes, or until just fork-tender.

3. Remove the potatoes from the oven and let cool for a few minutes. Spread 2 tablespoons of the oil over the entire surface of a 13- × 9-inch baking tray and place the potatoes on top.

4. Now comes the fun part! Using the palm of your hand or the underside of a small cup, smack the potatoes until they pop. You don't need to take out any inner anger on them; just squish them down a bit so they are somewhat flat but not pancaked. Drizzle the remaining 1 tablespoon of oil overtop and return them to the oven for 30 minutes. You won't need to flip them over, just lift them once so they don't stick.

5. Remove from the oven, dot some butter on each potato, garnish with a thyme sprig, and season to taste with salt and pepper. Return the potatoes to the oven for about 6 to 8 minutes, or until golden and crispy.

6. Remove from the oven and scatter the cheese evenly among the spuds. Give them another 4 to 5 minutes in the oven to melt the cheese.

7. Sprinkle with the paprika (if using).

Hasselback Potatoes

These wonderful cheesy, buttery, garlicky potatoes are a guaranteed hit if you are feeding a hungry crowd. They not only are fun to make but also look wonderful on a dinner plate. The thin cuts in the potato make for a soft center and crisp outer layer, giving you the best of both worlds when you are torn between the crispiness of a french fry and the smooth, creaminess of a baked potato.

SERVES 4

Here's what you'll need:

½ cup salted butter

5 whole garlic cloves, peeled

4 Yukon gold potatoes

3–4 rosemary sprigs, tied together by the stems

Kosher salt and ground black pepper

4 thyme sprigs

1–1½ cups grated Gruyère cheese

Here's how it's done:

1. In a saucepan over low heat, melt the butter with the garlic cloves sitting in it. Let sit for 1 hour, or up to 2 hours, warming the butter gently if it starts to solidify.

2. Preheat the oven to 375°F.

3. Scrub the potatoes to remove any dirt. Pat dry. Using an extremely sharp paring knife, cut equal slits along the length of each potato, going about three-quarters of the way through and keeping the potato intact. Your slices should be about ¼ inch apart, giving you 12 to 13 slits.

4. Place the potatoes in a 13- × 9-inch, lightly oiled baking dish. Dip the rosemary sprigs into the garlic butter and brush the potatoes generously with it.

5. Sprinkle liberally with kosher salt and pepper. Bake, uncovered, for 30 minutes.

6. Brush the potatoes with more butter and return them to the oven for 20 more minutes. Remove them from the oven again, place a thyme sprig on top of each potato, and sprinkle the cheese overtop. Return to the oven for 10 minutes, or until the cheese is totally melted and bubbly.

7. Serve immediately. Place any remaining garlic butter in a small dish and serve alongside the potatoes.

Spring Asparagus with Bagna Cauda

In this recipe, a refreshing splash of citrus plays off the earthy aromatics of the asparagus. It is simple to prepare and is sure to satisfy any happy lodge guest craving something fun with dinner.

SERVES 4

Here's what you'll need:

BAGNA CAUDA SAUCE:

2 tablespoons slivered almonds

6 tablespoons salted butter

2 tablespoons extra virgin olive oil, divided

5 garlic cloves, minced

2 teaspoons anchovy paste

1 oregano sprig

1 teaspoon grated lemon zest

1 teaspoon grated orange zest

2 tablespoons orange juice

1 tablespoon lemon juice

ASPARAGUS:

1½ lb asparagus, ends trimmed

Kosher salt and ground black pepper

Here's how it's done:

1. Preheat the oven to 350°F.

2. Place the slivered almonds on a baking sheet and toast in the oven for 10 to 12 minutes, or until golden brown. Turn them around the halfway mark to ensure they toast evenly. Set aside to cool. Turn up the oven to 425°F.

3. To make the sauce, in a saucepan over medium-low heat, melt the butter with 1 tablespoon of the oil. Add the garlic, anchovy paste, oregano, lemon zest, and orange zest and mix well. Pour in the orange juice and lemon juice and whisk gently to combine. Warm through for about 10 to 12 minutes, or until the garlic is fragrant and browning slightly and the sauce is completely blended. Remove from the heat and stir for a couple of minutes to keep it from separating.

4. Toss the asparagus with the remaining 1 tablespoon of oil and sprinkle with salt and pepper to taste. Place the asparagus on a baking tray and roast for 12 to 15 minutes, or until the stalks are fork-tender and starting to brown. Don't overcook them.

5. Transfer the asparagus to a serving platter. Pour the bagna cauda overtop and garnish with the toasted almonds for a grand finish.

Roast Cauliflower with Aromatic Spices

In this recipe, the humble cauliflower is the main attraction. The process of roasting it in unpretentious seasonings showcases its texture and overall taste, which are so often hidden under a heavy sauce. The smell of the spices toasting will make you feel better about being back in the kitchen after an epic day on the slopes.

SERVES 4

Here's what you'll need:

1 cauliflower

3 tablespoons extra virgin olive oil, divided

1 teaspoon grated lime zest

1 teaspoon curry powder (strength according to taste)

1 teaspoon ground turmeric

Kosher salt and ground black pepper

1 teaspoon coriander seeds

1 teaspoon mustard seeds (yellow or black)

1 teaspoon cumin seeds

Here's how it's done:

1. Preheat the oven to 425°F.

2. Wash the cauliflower thoroughly and cut it into 1-inch florets, discarding the core. You should have between 8 and 10 cups—it seems like a lot, but it will shrink once it begins to roast. Pat dry with a tea towel and place in a large bowl.

3. In a mixing bowl, whisk together 2 tablespoons of the oil with the lime zest, curry powder, turmeric, and salt and pepper to taste. Pour this over the cauliflower florets and toss gently to coat. Transfer the cauliflower to a 13- × 9-inch baking sheet.

4. Bake the cauliflower for 15 minutes. Remove from the oven and toss so that both sides are evenly roasted. Return to the oven for another 5 to 10 minutes, or until golden and fork-tender.

5. In a large skillet over high heat, place the remaining 1 tablespoon of oil and fry the coriander, mustard, and cumin seeds for 2 minutes, until they are toasty and fragrant.

6. Add the cauliflower to the skillet and toss it in the fried seeds. Serve straight from the skillet.

Steamed Broccoli with Mountain Flair

A kitchen staple like broccoli can be used in so many different recipes that it is on my "essentials" list. In this recipe, it is steamed and then paired with a savory and tangy sauce, bringing some mountain flair to this sublime vegetable.

SERVES 4

Here's what you'll need:

1 large bunch broccoli, washed and cut into florets

1 garlic clove, crushed

3 tablespoons extra virgin olive oil

2 tablespoons soy sauce

1–2 tablespoons liquid honey

1 tablespoon sesame oil

1 teaspoon balsamic vinegar

1-inch piece ginger, peeled

1 teaspoon ground turmeric

1 serrano chili, deseeded and diced

1 teaspoon black sesame seeds

Here's how it's done:

1. Fill a large saucepan with just over 1 inch of water and bring to a boil over high heat. Place a steamer basket over the water, add the broccoli florets, and cover with a lid. Turn down the heat to medium-low and steam, covered, for 5 minutes.

2. Remove from the heat and discard the steaming water. Allow the broccoli to drain for 1 to 2 minutes to get rid of any residual moisture and then transfer to a serving dish.

3. Meanwhile, in a mixing bowl, whisk together the garlic, olive oil, soy sauce, honey, sesame oil, and balsamic. Grate the ginger directly into the mixing bowl, add the turmeric, and mix to combine. Add the serrano chili—don't touch your eyes!—and whisk until all the ingredients are fully combined.

4. Pour the dressing over the broccoli and toss to evenly coat. Finish by scattering the black sesame seeds overtop for some drama.

Brussel Sprouts with Homemade Pesto

This dish has made an appearance at a lot of backcountry holidays. It can be found lounging around the buffet every Thanksgiving and reappears at Christmas—and it wouldn't dare miss Easter. However, don't feel you have to wait for a holiday or special occasion to put this on display, because it is one sociable and confident dish. One might even go so far as to say it's an extrovert.

SERVES 4

Here's what you'll need:

SPROUTS:

1 tablespoon salted butter

1 lb Brussels sprouts

Extra virgin olive oil

Kosher salt and ground black pepper

PESTO:

½ cup pine nuts

4 cups fresh basil leaves

2 garlic cloves, minced

1 ¼ cup extra virgin olive oil, plus extra

¼ cup grated Parmigiano-Reggiano cheese

Kosher salt and ground black pepper

½ lemon, juiced

Here's how it's done:

1. Preheat the oven to 375°F. Butter a 13- × 9-inch casserole dish. Prepare an ice bath.

2. Bring a large saucepan of lightly salted water to a boil over high heat. The Brussel sprouts should be completely covered in water while they cook.

3. Trim the ends of the sprouts and discard any outer leaves that look yucky. Give them a quick rinse to remove any dirt or debris.

4. Add the sprouts to the boiling water and blanch for 3 minutes. Immediately transfer them to the ice bath for about 30 seconds to shock them and stop the cooking process. Strain in a colander and let sit for 1 minute to release any excess moisture. Pat dry. On a cutting board, cut the larger sprouts in half and leave the smaller ones alone.

5. Place the sprouts in the prepared dish and drizzle with a touch of oil, pinch of salt, and pepper to taste.

6. Bake for 25 to 35 minutes, or until the outer leaves are golden brown and the sprouts are tender all the way through. Toss a couple of times while they are in the oven.

7. Meanwhile, make the pesto. Spread the pine nuts on a baking sheet and place them in the oven with the sprouts for 5 minutes. Remove from the oven and toss. Return to the oven for 3 to 5 minutes, until all the nuts are evenly golden brown. Remove from the oven and set aside to cool for a couple of minutes.

8. Place the basil in a food processor, removing any remaining stalks or unusable pieces. Pulse a couple of times and then add the pine nuts and garlic. This time, blend to combine. With the machine running, gradually pour in the oil to emulsify. Turn the machine off and add the cheese, and salt and pepper to taste. Drizzle in the lemon juice with the machine running on low and combine the ingredients until they produce a chunky sauce. You can add more olive oil, 1 tablespoon at a time, for an even creamier pesto, if you like.

9. Remove the sprouts from the oven and drizzle with the pesto, 1 tablespoon at a time, while they are nice and warm, using a spatula or large spoon to help roll them around and coat them evenly. You may not want to use all the pesto. (It stores beautifully in an airtight container in the fridge for a couple of days and can be used as a dip or spread.) I personally love to use a lot of it in this recipe.

10. Serve immediately. It's best not to keep this dish warm in the oven, as the pesto doesn't react well to the heat.

Linguine and Clam Sauce

Some of the best recipes are the ones that come to us from our relatives. This recipe was passed on to me by my mom. It is a family favorite, and we often enjoy it as an entrée with a warm baguette when we visit my mom. And of course, I always feel nostalgic when I make it for my own family.

SERVES 4

Here's what you'll need:

¼ cup salted butter

3 garlic cloves, minced

3 tablespoons chopped fresh flat-leaf parsley, plus extra for garnish

Ground black pepper

2 chicken bouillon cubes

1 (10 oz) can whole baby clams and juice

¾ cup dry white wine

1½ teaspoons lemon juice

¾ cup whipping (35–40%) cream

Kosher salt

14 oz linguine

Grated Parmigiano-Reggiano cheese, for serving (optional)

Here's how it's done:

1. In a large skillet over medium heat, melt the butter. Add the garlic, parsley, and pepper to taste. Using the back of a spoon, crush the bouillon cubes into the bottom of the pan and mix to combine with the other ingredients.

2. Add the clam juice, reserving the clams. Whisk to combine and then whisk in the wine and lemon juice. Add the cream and a large pinch of salt, and whisk again to combine. Bring to a boil, then turn down the heat to low. Add the whole baby clams and simmer, uncovered, for 10 to 15 minutes. Season to taste.

3. While the clams simmer, bring a large saucepan of heavily salted water to a boil over high heat. Cook the linguine in the boiling water for 11 to 13 minutes, or until al dente. Drain the pasta.

4. Cover the bottom of a serving dish with sauce. Add the pasta and toss lightly. Pour the rest of the sauce overtop and add a sprinkle of fresh parsley. Have a serving dish of grated Parmigiano-Reggiano on hand for personal service.

Asparagus Fries with Roasted Garlic Aioli

Going for fries and a pint after a day of spring skiing is a sweet way to end a day. And if those fries are made from asparagus instead of the usual suspects, you really have something to be excited about. This recipe is a fantastic après-ski indulgence, but it will most likely become a family favorite for just about any occasion.

SERVES 4

Here's what you'll need:

AIOLI:

1 head garlic, roasted (see note, page 65)

1 teaspoon extra virgin olive oil

1 cup full-fat mayonnaise

3–4 tablespoons lemon juice (1–2 lemons)

½ teaspoon red pepper flakes

Kosher salt

ASPARAGUS:

3 egg whites

1½ tablespoons full-fat mayonnaise

2 cups dried Italian breadcrumbs

½ cup grated Parmigiano-Reggiano cheese

2 tablespoons chopped fresh flat-leaf parsley

Kosher salt and ground black pepper

1 lb asparagus, ends trimmed

1 tablespoon extra virgin olive oil

Here's how it's done:

1. Squeeze the garlic cloves to remove the roasted pulp and, using a fork, mash it up in a mixing bowl. Add the oil and mayonnaise, mix to combine, and then whisk in the lemon juice, 1 tablespoon at a time, until you achieve a creamy and smooth sauce that coats the back of a wooden spoon. Add the red pepper flakes and a pinch of salt and mix to combine. Taste for seasoning. Some people like a lemony aioli and others prefer the garlic and mayonnaise to be the prime flavors.

2. To prepare the asparagus, preheat the oven to 350°F. Lightly oil two baking sheets. Have two shallow bowls at hand.

3. In a mixing bowl, whisk the egg whites with the mayonnaise until fully combined. Pour the mixture into one of the bowls.

4. In the second bowl, mix together the breadcrumbs, cheese, parsley, and salt and pepper to taste.

5. Roll each asparagus spear in the egg mixture and then dredge through the breadcrumb mixture.

6. Place the asparagus on the baking sheets about 1 inch apart and lightly drizzle with the 1 tablespoon of oil. Bake for 20 to 25 minutes, turning once, until golden and crispy.

7. Remove from the oven and let rest for a couple of minutes. Place on a platter and serve with the roasted garlic aioli on the side.

Seafood Pasta with Coconut Milk and Green Curry

Some of the people I worked with over the years always asked me to make this when they were on shift with me. It could be because they were living away from home for the first time and hadn't eaten a lot of prawns, scallops, or clams. Or it could be that the creaminess of the sauce coupled with the luxury of gorgeous seafood is too much to resist. Either way, I'm sure your own family and friends will be asking you to prepare this for them often as well.

SERVES 4–6

Here's what you'll need:

1 cup salted butter

1¼ cups all-purpose flour

3 cups whole (3.25%) milk, divided

2 (each 8 oz) packages brick-style cream cheese, cubed

3 garlic cloves, crushed

2 tablespoons green curry paste

2 tablespoons curry powder (strength according to taste)

2 (each 13.5 oz) cans full-fat coconut milk

1 lime, zested and juiced

½ bunch cilantro, coarsely chopped, plus extra for garnish

Kosher salt

½ (10 oz) can whole baby clams

½ (28 oz) can sweety drop peppers (see note)

12–14 oz dried penne

1½ tablespoons extra virgin olive oil, divided

½ lb scallops

½ lb prawns, peeled and deveined

1 yellow bell pepper, sliced

3–4 green onions, thinly sliced

Here's how it's done:

1. To make the sauce, in a large saucepan or Dutch oven over medium-low heat, melt the butter. Gradually whisk in the flour. There is no need to whisk vigorously—you just want the ingredients to combine. This sauce uses a slightly blond roux. It takes about 2 minutes for the flour to lose its raw smell and instead emit a slight nutty smell.

2. Gradually whisk in 2 cups of the milk until the sauce is nice and smooth. Add the cream cheese and pour the remaining 1 cup of milk overtop. Stirring constantly, let the cream cheese melt into the milk. Once all the cream cheese has melted, whisk in the garlic, curry paste, and curry powder, followed by the coconut milk. Add the lime zest and juice, cilantro, and a pinch of salt, and whisk gently to combine. Finally, add the baby clams, discarding about half of the juice. Add the sweety drop peppers, along with 2 tablespoons of the packed juice.

3. Keep the sauce simmering on low heat while you prepare the pasta and seafood, whisking occasionally.

4. Bring a large saucepan of heavily salted water to a boil over high heat. Add the penne and cook until al dente, 12 to 14 minutes. Drain and set aside for a few minutes. I often reserve some of the pasta water and pour it overtop to keep the pasta from drying out.

5. In a large skillet over medium-high heat, warm 1 tablespoon of the oil and fry the scallops for about 2 minutes per side. The scallops will have a ¼-inch golden-brown crust on each side and an opaque center. Remove from the pan and set aside.

6. Place the prawns and bell pepper in the same skillet, drizzle with the remaining ½ tablespoon of oil, and cook on medium-high heat until the prawns are pink on the outside and slightly opaque, about 1 to 2 minutes per side. Remove from the skillet and set aside.

7. I often serve this dish directly from the saucepan I cooked the pasta in, but if you have a nice large serving bowl, pour in enough sauce to cover the bottom. Add the pasta and pour the remaining sauce overtop. Add the scallops and prawns and toss a couple of times to evenly distribute throughout the pasta. Serve with a sprinkle of cilantro and the green onions.

NOTE: Sweety drop peppers are red Peruvian mini-peppers. These versatile little vegetables are just bigger than a pomegranate aril and are packed in a sweetened vinegar liquid. They are fabulous in this seafood pasta, of course, as well as in salads or various vegetable dishes. You can find them easily in many grocery stores.

Roasted Cremini Mushrooms and Asparagus with Miso and Pomegranate

I must admit that I am a huge fan of roasted anything, but cremini mushrooms, with their earthy aroma, coupled with fresh spring asparagus is a heavenly pairing. In this recipe, the fun begins after the roasting, with a tangy miso paste dressing and some vibrant pomegranate arils to add texture.

SERVES 4

Here's what you'll need:

2 lb cremini mushrooms (see note)

3 tablespoons extra virgin olive oil, divided

1 teaspoon kosher salt, divided

1 teaspoon ground black pepper

2–3 thyme sprigs

1 lb fresh asparagus, ends trimmed

2 garlic cloves, crushed

¼ cup white wine vinegar

2 tablespoons white or yellow miso paste

1 tablespoon vegetable oil

1 tablespoon smooth Dijon mustard

2 teaspoons granulated sugar

¼ cup fresh pomegranate arils

NOTE: When choosing mushrooms for this dish, make sure you pick firm, dry (not slimy or dried-out) ones with minimal flaws. Also, choose small and medium mushrooms rather than large ones. Cremini mushrooms are close cousins of the white mushroom but are often chosen over the white ones for their earthy and full flavor

Here's how it's done:

1. Preheat the oven to 375°F.

2. Wipe the mushrooms with a damp cloth or a mushroom brush. Trim the stems and place the mushrooms in a shallow baking dish or cast iron skillet large enough to hold them without crowding. Toss with 2 tablespoons of the oil, sprinkle with ½ teaspoon of the salt and all the pepper, and place the thyme sprigs on top. Roast for about 10 to 12 minutes and then remove from the oven. Pour out any released moisture (the reserved liquid can be used as a vegan stock) and return to the oven for 15 more minutes or until the mushrooms are fork-tender and evenly browned.

3. Add the asparagus to the roasted mushrooms and toss gently to mix everything around. Drizzle the remaining 1 tablespoon of oil overtop and return to the oven for another 15 to 20 minutes, or until the asparagus is just tender and browned slightly on the edges.

4. During the second round of roasting, prepare the miso paste dressing. In a bowl, whisk together the garlic, vinegar, miso paste, oil, Dijon, and sugar until combined and completely smooth. Add the remaining ½ teaspoon of salt and whisk again. Set aside.

5. Remove the mushrooms and asparagus from the oven and place them in a serving dish. Discard the thyme sprigs and spoon the miso paste dressing evenly overtop. Sprinkle generously with the pomegranate arils and serve immediately.

Chickpeas and Kale in Pomodoro Sauce

My colleagues and I serve many backcountry vegetarian dishes every day and are always on the lookout for new ideas to keep the vegetarian palate delighted. This terrific recipe is not only easy and affordable, it is also versatile and quick. The chickpeas and kale offer plenty of protein and pack a powerful punch of fiber and potassium. This dish is also portable enough to take for lunch on the trail.

SERVES 4

Here's what you'll need:

½ cup + 1 tablespoon extra virgin olive oil, divided

4 garlic cloves, minced

1 cooking onion, diced

1 (28 oz) can whole plum tomatoes

1½ teaspoons fennel seeds

1 teaspoon red pepper flakes

1 teaspoon dried oregano

1 teaspoon granulated sugar

Kosher salt and ground black pepper

2–3 cups chopped kale leaves

2 (each 15.5 oz) cans chickpeas, rinsed and drained

½ cup grated asiago cheese

6–8 fresh basil leaves, chiffonade

Here's how it's done:

1. In a saucepan over medium heat, warm ½ cup of oil and sauté the garlic and onion until fragrant and softened, about 3 to 4 minutes.

2. Pour the tomatoes and their juice into a mixing bowl and crush them with your hand, discarding any bits of stem. Add the tomatoes to the saucepan. Turn down the heat to medium-low.

3. Add the fennel seeds, red pepper flakes, oregano, sugar, and salt and pepper to taste. Mix to combine and cook on medium-low for 20 to 25 minutes, or until the sauce starts to thicken. Stir in the kale leaves. Continue to cook until the kale has wilted, about 2 to 3 minutes.

4. Add the chickpeas and the remaining 1 tablespoon of oil. Mix well.

5. Remove from the heat and serve in a tureen or individual serving bowls. Garnish with the asiago and a chiffonade of basil.

NOTE: This dish is wonderful on fluffed basmati rice or rice noodles, making it a gluten-free option as well.

Grown-Up Mac and Cheese with Chorizo

Nothing says comfort food like mac and cheese, but this recipe is one giant leap forward from the mac and cheese of your youth, thanks to the spicy kick of chorizo. It's definitely a lodge favorite and a wonderful side dish or entrée on a snowy evening meal.

SERVES 6–8

Here's what you'll need:

½ cup salted butter

¼ cup all-purpose flour

4–5 cups 2% milk, divided

¾ cup brick-style cream cheese, cubed

2 cups grated aged, sharp cheddar cheese

2 cups grated Swiss cheese

1 cup grated Gruyère cheese

1 teaspoon dried mustard

1 teaspoon paprika, plus extra for garnish

1 teaspoon ground nutmeg

½ teaspoon ground turmeric

½ teaspoon cayenne pepper

Kosher salt and ground black pepper

1½ lb dried penne

3 cooked chorizo sausages

2–3 cups whipping (35–40%) cream

Fresh flat-leaf parsley, for garnish

NOTE: This recipe is best made in a big, heavy-duty saucepan because of the amount of time it spends on the heat.

Here's how it's done:

1. In a large, heavy-bottomed saucepan over medium heat, melt the butter and swirl it around to cover the bottom of the pan. Whisk in the flour to make a nutty-smelling roux. It will take about 2 to 3 minutes for the flour to just begin to brown and all the butter and flour bits to be incorporated. Add 4 cups of the milk, 1 cup at a time, whisking well between additions.

2. Add the cream cheese, one cube at a time, whisking until smooth and completely integrated. If you feel that the sauce is too thick, gradually whisk in the remaining 1 cup of milk.

3. Add the cheddar and stir until completely melted. Add the Swiss cheese and stir until completely melted. Finally, add the Gruyère and stir until completely melted. (Yes, this step is a little bit repetitious.)

4. Add the dried mustard, paprika, nutmeg, turmeric, cayenne pepper, a pinch of salt, and pepper to taste. Stir until the sauce is a smooth and creamy. Turn down the heat to low.

5. Bring a large saucepan of heavily salted water to a boil over high heat. Cook the pasta until al dente, about 10 to 12 minutes. I like penne for this recipe because the cheese sauce gets right inside the noodle and coats the outside beautifully.

6. Slice the chorizo about a ¼ inch thick on the bias and then into half-moons for easier eating, then add to the sauce to warm through while the pasta is cooking.

7. Drain the pasta and add it directly to the sauce.

8. Stir in 2 cups of the cream and heat gently for 4 to 6 minutes, stirring occasionally, or until the pasta and sauce are both warm and have gotten to know one another. If the sauce is too thick, add the third cup of cream.

9. Garnish with paprika and a mound of coarsely chopped fresh parsley. I prefer to serve my mac and cheese right in the very same pot I made the sauce in so that I use fewer dishes.

Arancini with Vodka Marinara

Arancini, golden, crispy Italian rice balls, make for a terrific starter or side dish. In this recipe, the vodka marinara, buffalo mozzarella, and prosciutto stuffing inside these little treasures practically guarantees an everlasting food memory.

SERVES 4–6

Here's what you'll need:

RISOTTO:

4 cups chicken stock

2 tablespoons extra virgin olive oil

2 medium shallots, diced

2 garlic cloves, minced

1½ cups Arborio rice

¼ cup dry white wine

VODKA MARINARA:

1 (28 oz) can whole plum tomatoes

¼ cup extra virgin olive oil

6 garlic cloves, minced

½ teaspoon red pepper flakes

½ teaspoon dried oregano

Kosher salt and ground black pepper

¼ cup vodka

TO ASSEMBLE:

2 eggs

1½ cups dried breadcrumbs, divided

Kosher salt

½ cup grated Parmigiano-Reggiano cheese

2 tablespoons chopped fresh flat-leaf or curly parsley

¾ cup cubed buffalo mozzarella (15–16 cubes)

½ cup chopped prosciutto

4 cups vegetable oil, for frying

Fresh basil leaves, chiffonade, for garnish

Here's how it's done:

1. To make the risotto, in a saucepan set over medium-high heat, warm the stock. Turn down the heat to medium to keep it just warm.

2. In a skillet over medium heat, warm the oil and sauté the diced shallots and garlic for 3 minutes to soften a little. Add the rice and stir continuously for 2 minutes to toast and combine with the shallots and garlic. Add the wine and stir until it has been absorbed by the rice. Add the stock, about ½ cup at a time. Stir until each addition has been fully absorbed before adding the next one, stirring continuously. The risotto is finished when it is just tender all the way through, plump but still al dente. It will take about 20 minutes for the whole cooking process from beginning to end. You may not need all the stock. Set the risotto aside to cool completely.

3. To make the vodka marinara, place the tomatoes and their juice in a bowl and crush them with your hands, removing any stems. In a skillet over medium heat, warm the oil and sauté the garlic until it starts to brown, about 3 minutes. Add the tomatoes and ¼ cup of water. Stir to combine and then add the red pepper flakes, oregano, and a pinch each of salt and pepper. Bring to a simmer and reduce for about 20 minutes, until the sauce has begun to thicken. Stir in the vodka and simmer for about 5 to 8 more minutes. Let cool completely and then pour into a serving bowl.

4. To assemble the arancini, beat the eggs in a large mixing bowl. Mix in ⅔ cup of the breadcrumbs, the kosher salt, cheese, and parsley. Add the cooled rice and, using a wooden spoon or your hands, mix to combine everything well.

5. Form the rice mixture into 15 or 16 rice balls, about 1½ inches in diameter.

6. Using your thumb, make an indentation in each ball and stuff with a cube of mozzarella and some prosciutto. Roll the rice around the stuffing to reshape the ball and set aside on a plate. Continue with the remaining rice, mozzarella, and prosciutto.

7. In a large, deep saucepan over medium-high heat, bring the 4 cups of oil to 350°F. If you don't have an oil or candy thermometer, simply place a wooden spoon, handle down, in the hot oil. If bubbles form around the handle where it meets the oil and the oil is also rippling slightly, you are good to go.

8. Roll the balls in the remaining breadcrumbs, shaking off any excess. Working in batches, use a slotted spoon or deep-frying basket to lower the balls into the hot oil. Gently swirl the arancini a couple of times as they fry to ensure even frying and a gorgeous golden glow. This should take about 6 to 8 minutes per ball. Make sure to check the oil is frying at an even temperature between batches. Adjust the heat accordingly.

9. Remove from the pot and place on a wire rack set over a baking sheet to catch any drips of oil.

10. For presentation, it is nice to put the vodka marinara in a little bowl. Place this bowl on a serving platter and arrange the arancini around it. Sprinkle the arancini and the marinara with the fresh basil.

Chilled Sweet and Sour Zucchini with Mini Bell Peppers

This dish is a great one to pack in your lunch and take on the trail with you. It is a wonderful calorie replacer, as it doesn't contain anything that will slow you down. The zucchini is delicious chilled, so it is fine in your backpack even on the coldest winter day.

SERVES 4–6

Here's what you'll need:

3 green zucchini

4 mini bell peppers (a mix of colors is nice)

½ red onion

½ cup liquid honey or agave nectar

½ cup white wine vinegar

⅓ cup canola oil

2 garlic cloves, minced

1 teaspoon fresh thyme leaves

½ teaspoon red pepper flakes

Kosher salt and ground black pepper

Paprika (any type), for garnish

Here's how it's done:

1. Wash and pat dry the zucchini and bell peppers. Cut the zucchini into ½-inch ovals. Slice the bell peppers into quarters and discard the seeds. Slice the onion into pieces the same size as the bell pepper quarters. Toss the vegetables together in a medium mixing bowl.

2. In a small mixing bowl, mix together the honey, vinegar, and oil. Whisk in the garlic, thyme, red pepper flakes, and salt and pepper to taste. Pour the vinaigrette over the vegetables, tossing to coat everything evenly. Cover and place in the fridge for a couple of hours, or up to overnight.

3. Remove the bowl from the fridge and drain off the marinade. You can reserve it for another time if you want to have a quick vinaigrette on hand. (It will keep in an airtight container in the fridge for about 3 days.)

4. Transfer the vegetables to a serving dish and sprinkle lightly with paprika before serving.

Acknowledgments

I am often asked what backcountry cooking is, and the answer is often not as straightforward as I would hope. The heroes of the story often play as big a part in the final dish and experience as the food does. Plus, there's the complexity of keeping the pantry stocked in remote locations in the first place. For this reason I must acknowledge the humble talents of the Alpine Helicopter pilots, the cowboys and cowgirls who packed and unpacked thousands of pounds of food meticulously onto horses and mules, and the undeniable determination of the ridiculously skilled snowmobilers who make the remote journey in all kinds of weather, including in whiteouts. And the loaders and unloaders, for your strength and thousands of steps from helicopter, horse, or snow machine to the kitchen, making sure not an egg is cracked or a bag of spring mix is frozen.

To all the dedicated and inspiring lodge staff who I have worked with for over two decades and who made me laugh, cry, dance, and explore—you are my spirit animals. I have learned so much from all of you and wouldn't want to have a late-night kitchen party without any of you!

Thank you to the mad talent at Appetite: publisher Robert McCullough and publishing manager Lindsay Paterson, for your warm and welcoming personalities and shared vision. To my editor, Zoe Maslow, and associate editor, Katherine Stopa, for pushing me in all the right directions, ever so gently and ever so patiently. To Five Seventeen, for having the vision and the coolest name ever. To the sales, marketing, and production teams, for their hard work. And to everyone, for their understanding that sometimes I was off-grid and unable to respond—both a blessing and a curse in the backcountry, especially when you are trying to get to the finish line.

A very special thank-you to Hilary McMahon, my agent, for your early belief in me and for seeing what was possible. You are an absolute gem.

Heartfelt thanks to Catherine Strongman for guidance, encouragement, and continued support.

Gratitude to Shallon Cunningham of Salt Food Photo, Sylvia Kong, Noel Rogers, Roger Laurilla, and Paul Zizka. You took what was in my head and put it out there for the world to see. Just gorgeous.

I will never forget the test kitchen at the Paintbox Lodge in Canmore, Alberta. From the bottom of my heart, thank you to Mallory Deyne for your input, output, endurance, and pear coolers. To Sara Renner, Thomas Grandi, and the whole Paintbox team, you are all incredibly generous, immensely supportive, and terrific eaters.

To Roger and Loree of Battle Abbey; Cindy and Dave of Mistaya Lodge; Andre, Karin, Claude, and Annick of Assiniboine Lodge; Chris, Joanne, Sara, and Thomas of Talus Lodge; and Jackie Mah of Purcell Lodge. I can't thank you all enough for finding the most gorgeous photographs of your lodges and for sharing your piece of heaven with my readers.

A warm and humble thank-you to the incredible guests who have made the journey to these backcountry locations and who have encouraged me in the kitchen with their kindness, appetites, repeat pilgrimages, and enduring loyalty to all of the recipes.

And finally, to my family. The days, weeks, months away from everyone or all together at the lodges have taught us that we can make a life doing what we love. Lodge work is both selfish and selfless. It has taught us to become independent and to always put the needs of others above our own. I like to believe we are unique in our strengths and abilities and that our experiences have enriched our day-to-day lives with countless gifts and memories. You are the first, perfect snowflake of winter, the rainbow out the kitchen window, the beautiful and fragile yellow light that exudes from the branches of the fall larch trees—you are my everything.

Index